UNF#CK M
MIRACLE

UNF#CK MORNING MIRACLE HABITS

Pranshu Anand

The Readers Paradise
New Delhi - 110002

UNF#CK MORNING MIRACLE HABITS
Pranshu Anand

ISBN - 978-93-5977-910-2

Published by The Readers Paradise
thereadersparadisesales@gmail.com

Printed and bound by CPI Group (UK) Ltd, Croydon, CR0 4YY

Cover Design by Kamini Bijoria

Typeset by The Readers Paradise

First Edition: 2024

MIX
Paper | Supporting responsible forestry
FSC® C013604

Contents

Preface

Welcome to the book that's here to disrupt your mornings and, in turn, your life. If you've ever heard the advice that waking up early and having a "perfect" morning routine is the golden ticket to success, you might have thought, That's great... for someone else. For years, that was me too. I read all the articles, watched the videos, and tried my hand at creating an Instagram-worthy routine, only to find myself back in bed, hitting snooze, and feeling frustrated with myself for not sticking to it. It wasn't until I took a hard look at what was really blocking my progress that I found the key to true transformation.

This book isn't about giving you a step-by-step formula for a perfect morning, nor is it about waking up at 5 a.m. with a smile on your face every day. Real change isn't picture-perfect, and neither are mornings. This book is about breaking down the myths, the fears, and the unrealistic expectations that have held you back from creating a routine that actually works for you. It's about unfucking your morning by stripping away the fluff, getting real about the challenges, and giving you tools to create a routine that feels like freedom, not obligation.

When we think about transforming our lives, mornings often feel like the last place we want to start. After all, mornings are when we're groggy, tempted by the snooze button, and, let's face it, not in the mood for grand resolutions. But mornings are powerful because they're a blank slate, a chance to create momentum for the day ahead. Whether you're a student, a parent, an entrepreneur, or just someone who feels like you're constantly playing catch-up, there's magic in taking control of your morning.

In these pages, we're going to dive into the art and science of building a morning routine that's unique to you. We'll look at practical, research-backed techniques and break down common obstacles with a healthy dose of honesty and humor. You'll learn to work with your own rhythms, embrace progress over perfection, and redefine what success in the morning looks like. You'll learn to unfuck your mornings by unfucking the beliefs and habits that have held you back for too long.

This book is an invitation to break free from the routine that doesn't fit, to discard any preconceived notions about what a successful morning "should" look like, and to create mornings that genuinely set you up for a successful day-and life.

So, here's to mornings on your terms. Here's to breaking down barriers, creating habits that stick, and embracing a little bit of chaos along the way. Here's to every imperfect, resilient, powerful morning from here on out.

Let's get started.

Introduction

What if I told you that the first few moments of your day hold the power to reshape your life? For a long time, I believed mornings were just the prelude to the “real” part of the day, a groggy period to stumble through until coffee kicked in. But over time—and after a series of failed attempts at adopting the “perfect” morning routine—I learned that the morning isn’t just about what you do; it’s about who you become when you start the day with intention, honesty, and the right mindset.

This book is for those who are tired of cookie-cutter advice and the pressure to conform to some idealized, flawless morning routine. If you’re like most people, you’ve tried to wake up earlier, hit the gym, meditate, and knock out a long list of tasks before breakfast—all while feeling like you’re forcing yourself into a routine that doesn’t quite fit. And when things don’t go perfectly? It’s easy to feel like you’ve failed. The cycle of starting and stopping, of making progress and then slipping back, is exhausting. But what if there's a different way?

The goal of this book is simple: to help you create mornings that work for *you*. I'm here to challenge the myths around morning routines and help you craft a start to your day that feels empowering rather than rigid. This book isn't about waking up at a specific hour, nor is it about checking off a list of "must-do" activities. Instead, it's about unfucking your morning by facing your unique barriers, discarding what doesn't serve you, and embracing an approach that's flexible, realistic, and genuinely impactful.

In these pages, you'll find insights into the psychological and emotional obstacles that make mornings feel like a struggle. You'll learn that motivation doesn't always show up when you want it to, that perfection is the enemy of progress, and that consistency is built through resilience rather than rigor. You'll discover the power of creating a morning routine that's adaptable—one that evolves with your life rather than imposing itself on it.

We'll break down each element of a transformative morning routine, from waking up with purpose to incorporating habits that nourish your mind, body, and soul. I'll guide you through actionable steps for mastering the basics, and then we'll go deeper, addressing the common pitfalls and mental blocks that so often lead to abandoned routines. This book is as much about self-compassion as it is about self-discipline. It's about approaching each morning as an opportunity, not an obligation.

Whether you're a lifelong night owl, someone who craves structure but struggles to stick with it, or simply curious about how small changes in the morning can ripple into lifelong success, this book is for you.

Get ready to reclaim your mornings on your own terms. Get ready to make mornings the most powerful, resilient, and energizing part of your day—without the pressure, without the perfectionism, and without the excuses.

It's time to unlock success with every sunrise.

1 The Power of Mornings

There's something magical about the start of a new day. It's a fresh canvas, a new beginning, and a world of possibilities. Today, we're diving into "The Power of Mornings" and how transforming your mornings can set you on the path to lifelong success. So grab your coffee (or tea, if that's your thing), and let's explore how those early hours can become your secret weapon for a happier, more productive life.

Why Mornings Matter

Have you ever wondered why so many successful people swear by their morning routines? From CEOs to athletes, the world's top performers often credit their success to how they start their day. The quiet and calm of the early hours offer a unique opportunity to focus, reflect, and set the tone for the rest of your day. Here's why mornings matter so much:

1. **Mental Clarity:** After a good night's sleep, your mind is at its freshest in the morning. This clarity allows you to think more clearly, make better decisions, and tackle complex tasks with ease.
2. **Productivity Boost:** Early risers often get a head start on their day. With fewer distractions, you can knock out important tasks before the world wakes up, giving you a sense of accomplishment that fuels your motivation.
3. **Positive Mindset:** Starting your day with intention and positivity can set the tone for the entire day. It's like planting a seed of positivity that grows as the day progresses.
4. **Time for Yourself:** Mornings can be a time to focus on you. Whether it's exercise, meditation, reading, or just sipping your coffee in peace, those early hours can be a sanctuary for self-care.

Crafting Your Perfect Morning Routine

Creating a morning routine that works for you is all about finding balance and incorporating activities that set you up for success. Here's a step-by-step guide to crafting your perfect morning:

1. **Wake Up Early:** This might be the hardest part, especially if you're not a natural early riser. But even just 30 minutes earlier can make a big difference. Gradually adjust your

wake-up time by 10-15 minutes until you reach your desired time.

2. **Hydrate:** After hours of sleep, your body needs water. Start your day with a glass of water to kickstart your metabolism and rehydrate your body.
3. **Move Your Body:** Physical activity in the morning can boost your energy levels and improve your mood. It doesn't have to be a full workout; even a short walk, stretching, or yoga can make a big difference.
4. **Mindfulness Practice:** Spend a few minutes in meditation, deep breathing, or journaling. This helps clear your mind and set positive intentions for the day.
5. **Healthy Breakfast:** Fuel your body with a nutritious breakfast. Choose foods that give you sustained energy, like whole grains, fruits, and protein.
6. **Plan Your Day:** Take a few minutes to review your schedule and set your priorities. This helps you stay organized and focused throughout the day.

Real-Life Morning Routines of Successful People

Let's take a peek into the morning routines of some successful individuals to see how they leverage the power of mornings:

1. **Tim Cook, CEO of Apple:** Tim Cook wakes up at 3:45 a.m. and starts his day by checking emails for an hour. He then heads to the gym for a workout before grabbing a coffee and heading to the office.

2. **Oprah Winfrey, Media Mogul:** Oprah's morning routine includes meditation and exercise. She also spends time with her dogs and enjoys a healthy breakfast before starting her workday.
3. **Tony Robbins, Motivational Speaker:** Tony Robbins starts his day with a breathing exercise called "priming," followed by a cold shower and a workout. He believes these activities help him stay focused and energized.

Overcoming Common Morning Challenges

Even with the best intentions, mornings can be challenging. Here's how to overcome some common hurdles:

1. **Difficulty Waking Up:** If you struggle to wake up early, try adjusting your bedtime gradually. Create a relaxing bedtime routine to signal to your body that it's time to wind down.
2. **Lack of Time:** If mornings feel rushed, prepare the night before. Lay out your clothes, pack your lunch, and organize your to-do list to save time in the morning.
3. **Motivation:** On those days when you lack motivation, remind yourself of the benefits of a morning routine. Sometimes, just starting with one small activity, like stretching or journaling, can kickstart your day.

The Science Behind Morning Routines

Did you know that there's actual science behind why morning routines work? Here are a few key insights:

1. **Circadian Rhythms:** Your body's internal clock, or circadian rhythm, naturally aligns with the sunrise and sunset. Aligning your routine with these rhythms can enhance your energy levels and mood.
2. **Hormonal Balance:** In the morning, your body releases cortisol, a hormone that helps you wake up and feel alert. A consistent morning routine can help regulate this hormone and improve your overall well-being.
3. **Habit Formation:** According to research, it takes about 21 days to form a new habit. By consistently following a morning routine, you can create positive habits that become second nature.

Small Steps for Big Changes

You don't need to overhaul your entire morning routine overnight. Start with small, manageable changes and gradually build up. Here are a few simple ideas to get you started:

1. **Gratitude Journaling:** Spend a few minutes each morning writing down three things you're grateful for. This simple practice can shift your mindset to a more positive outlook.
2. **Mindful Eating:** Instead of rushing through breakfast, take the time to savor each bite. This can improve your digestion and help you start the day more mindfully.
3. **Digital Detox:** Avoid checking your phone first thing in the morning. Instead, focus on activities that nurture your mind and body.
4. **Personal Development:** Use your mornings to invest in yourself. Read a book, listen to a

podcast, or take an online course to learn something new.

Embracing Flexibility

While a consistent morning routine is beneficial, it's also important to be flexible. Life happens, and some mornings won't go as planned. That's okay! The key is to get back on track without feeling guilty. Remember, the goal is progress, not perfection.

Your Turn: Rise and Shine!

Now it's your turn to harness the power of mornings. Start by identifying one or two changes you can make to your current routine. Remember, the goal is to create a morning that energizes and inspires you. It's about finding what works best for you and sticking with it.

Mornings are a gift. They're a chance to set the tone for the rest of your day and, ultimately, your life. By embracing a mindful and intentional morning routine, you can unlock a new level of productivity, happiness, and success.

So, what will you do with your mornings? How will you rise and shine? The power is in your hands. Here's to transforming your mornings and, in turn, transforming your life. Cheers to new beginnings and the endless possibilities that each morning brings!

2 Unfuck Your Morning: Breaking Barriers to Real Change

There's no shortage of advice on how to craft the "perfect" morning routine. Tips about meditation, exercise, and affirmations abound, with promises of life-changing results if you can just muster the motivation to rise with the sun. But what if you're just *not* a morning person? What if the early hours feel like a personal battle, filled with resistance, excuses, and frustration?

If you're tired of feeling like you're losing the morning game before you even start, it's time to take a different approach. It is about getting real with yourself, confronting the barriers to a consistent morning routine, and breaking free from limiting beliefs and unrealistic expectations. In other words, it's time to unfuck your morning—one empowered, authentic step at a time.

Acknowledging the Blocks: Why Mornings Feel Hard for Many

Transforming your mornings isn't just about waking up earlier. It's about tackling the deeply ingrained beliefs and emotional hurdles that make mornings a struggle. Many of us have internalized stories that reinforce why we're "just not morning people" or why routines don't work for us. Here are some of the biggest blocks to a productive, fulfilling morning routine:

The Myth of "Not Being a Morning Person"

If you've ever thought, "I'm not a morning person." This phrase is deeply embedded in our culture, but what does it really mean? Science shows that while some people have natural preferences for different times of day (chronotypes), most of us can adapt our bodies to earlier routines with the right approach. The struggle, then, is not genetic or permanent—it's mind game.

When we label ourselves as "not morning person," we're putting up a barrier before we even try. Instead, try reframing this label. Think of yourself as someone who *can* thrive in the morning, with the right preparation and approach. Shifting your mindset is the first step to unfucking your morning.

Fear of Failure: The Cycle of Trying and Quitting

Many people set out to create a powerful morning routine but fall off track when things don't go as planned. Maybe you start strong but miss a few days, and soon enough, you abandon the routine altogether. This fear of failure—a feeling that you won't stick with it or can't meet your own standards—can be one of the biggest hurdles.

Unfucking your morning is about rejecting this cycle of guilt. Recognize that failing to follow through on your morning routine does *not* make you a failure. Instead, see each morning as a fresh opportunity. The point isn't to be flawless; it's to be resilient and keep coming back.

Perfectionism Paralysis: The Ideal Morning Doesn't Exist

Many of us fall into the trap of envisioning a "perfect" morning routine: rising before dawn, meditating, journaling, working out, and reading—all before 8 a.m. When we fall short of this ideal, it's easy to feel disappointed and abandon the routine altogether. But here's the thing: the perfect morning doesn't exist.

Perfectionism is often a disguise for fear—fear that if we can't do it perfectly, we shouldn't do it at all. To unfuck your morning, you need to let go of perfectionism and embrace a flexible, sustainable approach. The goal is not to live up to some ideal but to find a routine that feels right for *you*, flaws and all.

Real Talk: Stop Waiting for Motivation

One of the most common misconceptions about creating a morning routine is that it requires constant motivation. You might think you need to feel excited, energized, or inspired to get out of bed and start your day with purpose. But the truth is, waiting for motivation is a trap. Motivation is fickle and often doesn't show up until you've already taken the first step.

The Science of Action Over Emotion

Psychologists have found that action often precedes emotion. In other words, the feeling of motivation usually comes *after* you've started doing something, not before. This is why it's crucial to rely on action rather than waiting to feel ready. Even if you're tired, uninspired, or tempted to snooze, committing to a small action can kickstart your day.

Practical Tips to Get Moving

- **Use the 5-Minute Rule:** If the idea of a full routine feels overwhelming, commit to just five minutes. Often, getting started is the hardest part, and once you begin, you'll naturally keep going.
- **Plan the Night Before:** Set out your clothes, prepare a water bottle, or set up a coffee maker the night before. By reducing friction points, you're making it easier to get going without relying on motivation.
- **Anchor Your Routine with a Reward:** Find something that you look forward to in the morning, whether it's a hot cup of coffee, a delicious breakfast, or a few minutes of quiet journaling. Having a reward can help you look forward to mornings, even on tough days.

Reframing Perfection: Embracing Messy Mornings

The perfect morning routine is a fantasy. Some days, you'll hit snooze; other days, you'll feel rushed.

And that's okay. The process of building a morning habit is about showing up, even if it's messy, imperfect, or incomplete.

Permission to Be Imperfect

The beauty of a morning routine is not in its perfection but in its consistency. Give yourself permission to be imperfect. If you miss a day or skip a step, let it go and start fresh the next morning. Progress is built on imperfect, consistent action, not flawless execution.

Tracking Consistency Over Perfection

Instead of focusing on each individual day, track your consistency over time. How many days did you show up, even if it wasn't perfect? Aim for progress, not perfection. The goal is to build a habit that evolves with you, one that can bend without breaking.

Celebrating Small Wins

One of the best ways to reinforce your progress is by celebrating small wins. If you managed to wake up on time, completed one part of your routine, or simply avoided the snooze button, recognize that as a victory. These small moments of progress add up over time and keep you motivated on the journey.

Breaking Free from Social Expectations

Social media is full of "ideal" morning routines that show people meditating by sunrise, doing yoga, and drinking green juice. While these images can be inspiring, they often set unrealistic standards. Remember: your morning routine is for *you*. It doesn't need to look like anyone else's, and it doesn't need to be "Instagrammable."

Craft a Routine that Reflects You

The best morning routine is one that aligns with your unique lifestyle, values, and goals. Take the time to experiment with different activities and see what feels right for you. Maybe you prefer a quick workout to a long meditation session. Or perhaps reading energizes you more than journaling. The key is to create a morning routine that feels authentic and sustainable for you.

Silencing the Noise of Comparison

It's easy to fall into the trap of comparing your routine to others. Remember, social media is a highlight reel, not reality. The goal is not to keep up with anyone else's routine but to create one that resonates with you. Be intentional about blocking out the noise, and remind yourself that your journey is unique.

Embrace Progress Over Perfection

The journey of building a morning routine is never linear. Some days will feel easy and natural; other days will be a challenge. To unfuck your morning routine, you need to embrace the idea of progress over perfection. The goal is not to create a flawless routine but to develop a habit that is adaptable, resilient, and capable of evolving with you over time.

Starting Small for Sustainable Change

If you're trying to overhaul your morning all at once, it's easy to feel overwhelmed and give up. Instead, start small. Focus on one or two habits, and build gradually. Starting small makes it easier to stick with your routine and reduces the pressure to be perfect from day one.

Reflect and Adjust as Needed

Take time each week to reflect on what's working and what's not. Are there parts of your routine that feel forced or unhelpful? Don't be afraid to make adjustments. A morning routine is a living thing; it should grow and change with you. Flexibility is key to making it sustainable over the long term.

Unfucking Tips for Consistent Success

Ready to take your morning routine to the next level? Here are some straightforward, no-nonsense tips to help you create a consistent routine that works for you:

Set a Bedtime Alarm

Your morning routine actually begins the night before. Set a bedtime alarm as a reminder to start winding down, so you get enough rest to unfuck your morning. A well-rested mind and body are essential for any morning routine.

Habit Stacking

Habit stacking is a technique where you attach a new habit to an existing one, creating a chain of positive actions. For example, you could drink a glass of water right after brushing your teeth. By stacking your habits, you create a flow that makes it easier to follow through on each part of your routine.

Create a Reward System

Rewards can be a powerful motivator. Create a system where you reward yourself for sticking with your routine. This could be as simple as enjoying a favorite snack, treating yourself to a new book, or taking extra time for a relaxing activity. Rewards reinforce consistency and give you something to look forward to.

Practice Self-Compassion

Building a morning routine is a process, and you're bound to face setbacks along the way. Practice self-compassion by forgiving yourself when things don't go as planned. Beating yourself up for missing a day or two won't help; it only reinforces negative feelings. Instead, acknowledge the setback, and keep moving forward.

Embrace Flexibility

Life is unpredictable, and not every morning will go according to plan. Flexibility is the key to maintaining your routine in the long run. Some days you may need to adjust, cut back, or adapt based on circumstances. Remember, the goal is progress, not rigidity.

Bringing It All Together

Unfucking your morning is about freedom—freedom from limiting beliefs, perfectionism, and external expectations. It's about creating a morning routine that aligns with *your* values, *your* goals, and *your* unique rhythm. Every sunrise is an opportunity, a fresh start to create a day that reflects who you want to be.

Take that first step. Let go of the excuses and embrace the idea of messy, resilient mornings. With each sunrise, you're one step closer to the life you're envisioning. Unlock the power of every morning, and make it your own.

3 Mastering the Art of the Snooze-Proof Wake Up

If you're like most people, the snooze button is your best friend and worst enemy. It's a sweet, tempting siren song luring you back into the cozy embrace of your bed. But what if I told you there's a way to break free from the snooze cycle and wake up feeling refreshed and ready to conquer the day? Today, we're diving into "Mastering the Art of the Snooze-Proof Wake Up." So, let's get started on making those early hours your favorite part of the day.

Why Do We Love the Snooze Button?

Before we tackle the solution, let's understand the problem. Why is the snooze button so irresistible?

1. **Comfort and Warmth:** Let's face it, your bed is warm and comfortable, especially when the alarm goes off. Hitting snooze feels like granting yourself a little more time in paradise.
2. **Interrupted Sleep:** The sound of the alarm jolts you out of a deep sleep cycle, making you feel groggy and disoriented. Snoozing seems like a way to ease into the waking world.
3. **Lack of Motivation:** If you're not looking forward to the day ahead, it's easy to delay getting out of bed. The snooze button becomes a form of procrastination.
4. **Habitual Behavior:** Over time, hitting the snooze button can become a habit. Your brain gets used to those extra 5-10 minutes of sleep, making it harder to break the cycle.

The Consequences of Snoozing

While it might feel good in the moment, hitting snooze has several downsides:

1. **Fragmented Sleep:** Those extra minutes of sleep are usually fragmented and low-quality, leaving you feeling more tired.
2. **Increased Stress:** Waking up multiple times can trigger a stress response, making you start your day on edge.
3. **Reduced Productivity:** A chaotic morning can set a negative tone for the rest of the day, reducing your overall productivity and focus.
4. **Health Impact:** Chronic sleep disruption can lead to long-term health issues, including cardiovascular problems and weakened immune function.

Strategies for a Snooze-Proof Wake-Up

Now that we know why we snooze and the downsides of it, let's explore some practical strategies to master the art of the snooze-proof wake up.

1. **Create a Bedtime Routine:** A consistent bedtime routine helps signal to your body that it's time to wind down. This can include activities like reading, taking a warm bath, or practicing relaxation techniques.
2. **Set a Consistent Wake-Up Time:** Try to wake up at the same time every day, even on weekends. This helps regulate your body's internal clock and makes it easier to wake up naturally.
3. **Optimize Your Sleep Environment:** Ensure your bedroom is conducive to sleep. This means a cool, dark, and quiet environment. Invest in a comfortable mattress and pillows to enhance your sleep quality.
4. **Limit Screen Time Before Bed:** The blue light from screens can interfere with your sleep. Try to avoid screens at least an hour before bedtime. Instead, engage in relaxing activities that don't involve electronics.
5. **Use a Gradual Alarm Clock:** Instead of a jarring alarm, consider using a gradual alarm clock that simulates a sunrise. This can help you wake up more naturally and reduce the temptation to hit snooze.
6. **Place Your Alarm Clock Out of Reach:** If your alarm clock is within arm's reach, it's easy to hit snooze. Placing it across the room forces you to get out of bed to turn it off.

7. **Practice Good Sleep Hygiene:** Avoid caffeine and heavy meals close to bedtime. Engage in calming activities in the evening and create a bedtime ritual that helps you unwind.
8. **Incorporate Morning Rituals You Enjoy:** If you have something to look forward to in the morning, it can make getting out of bed easier. This could be a delicious breakfast, a favorite podcast, or a morning walk.

Building Motivation to Wake Up

Motivation is a key factor in mastering the snooze-proof wake up. Here are some tips to boost your motivation:

1. **Set Clear Goals:** Having clear, achievable goals can give you a sense of purpose and make you excited to start your day. Write down your goals and review them each morning.
2. **Visualize Your Success:** Spend a few minutes each night visualizing your ideal morning and how it will set you up for a successful day. This mental practice can increase your motivation to get up.
3. **Create a Vision Board:** A vision board with images and quotes that inspire you can be a powerful motivator. Place it somewhere you'll see it every morning to remind you of your aspirations.
4. **Accountability Partner:** Find a friend or family member who also wants to wake up earlier. Hold each other accountable and check in regularly to share your progress and challenges.
5. **Reward Yourself:** Set up a reward system for waking up on time. Treat yourself to something

you enjoy, like a special breakfast or a leisurely morning activity, as a reward for not hitting snooze.

The Power of Habit

Habits are powerful tools for creating lasting change. Here's how to build a habit of waking up without hitting snooze:

1. **Start Small:** Begin by setting your alarm 10-15 minutes earlier than usual. Gradually increase the time as you get used to waking up earlier.
2. **Consistency is Key:** Be consistent with your wake-up time, even on weekends. This helps reinforce the habit and makes it easier to wake up naturally.
3. **Track Your Progress:** Keep a journal to track your wake-up times and how you feel each day. Reflecting on your progress can boost your motivation and help you stay committed.
4. **Stay Positive:** Focus on the benefits of waking up early rather than the challenges. Celebrate your successes and don't be too hard on yourself if you slip up occasionally.

Real-Life Success Stories

Let's hear from a few people who've successfully mastered the snooze-proof wake up:

1. **Emily, Marketing Manager:** "I used to hit snooze multiple times and felt groggy all morning. By placing my alarm clock across the room and creating a relaxing bedtime routine, I've been able to wake up on time and start my day with energy."

2. **Jake, Fitness Enthusiast:** "Waking up early for my workouts was tough at first. But once I started using a gradual alarm clock and set up a morning playlist I love, it became much easier. Now, I can't imagine my mornings without my exercise routine."
3. **Lily, Stay-at-Home Mom:** "As a mom, I needed those extra minutes of sleep, but it was making my mornings chaotic. I started waking up 30 minutes earlier and used that time for myself—meditation and a cup of tea. It's made a world of difference in how I handle the day."

Overcoming Common Challenges

Even with the best intentions, there will be challenges. Here's how to overcome some common obstacles:

- **Inconsistent Sleep Schedule:** If your schedule varies, it can be hard to wake up consistently. Try to maintain a regular bedtime and wake-up time as much as possible, even with a busy schedule.
- **Nighttime Disruptions:** If you're frequently waking up during the night, it can make mornings harder. Evaluate your sleep environment and habits to identify and address potential disruptions.
- **Low Energy Levels:** If you're struggling with low energy in the morning, consider adjusting your diet and exercise routine. Eating a balanced diet and incorporating regular physical activity can improve your overall energy levels.

Embrace the Morning Challenge

Waking up without hitting snooze is a challenge, but it's one worth embracing. By making small changes and staying committed, you can transform your mornings and, ultimately, your life. Remember, the goal is progress, not perfection. Celebrate your successes and learn from your setbacks.

Mornings are a fresh start, a new beginning each day. By mastering the art of the snooze-proof wake-up, you can seize those early hours and set a positive tone for the rest of your day. So, let's unfuck morning together, embracing the power of a snooze-free morning and unlocking our full potential. Here's to a bright and energetic start to each new day!

4 The Science of Sleep

Have you ever wondered why we spend about a third of our lives sleeping? It turns out that sleep is much more than just a time for rest—it's a crucial component of our overall well-being. Today, we're diving into "The Science of Sleep" to uncover the mysteries of why we sleep, what happens when we do, and how understanding sleep can transform your mornings and your life. So, grab a comfy seat, maybe a cozy blanket, and let's explore the fascinating world of sleep.

Why Do We Sleep?

Let's start with the basics: why do we sleep? Despite decades of research, scientists are still unraveling all the mysteries of sleep, but we do know some key reasons why it's so important:

1. **Restoration:** Sleep helps repair and rejuvenate our bodies. During deep sleep, your body releases growth hormones, repairs tissues, and builds muscle and bone.
2. **Brain Function:** Sleep is essential for cognitive functions like memory, learning, and problem-solving. It helps your brain process and store information from the day.
3. **Emotional Well-being:** Adequate sleep is crucial for emotional regulation. It helps you manage stress, anxiety, and mood swings.
4. **Immune System Support:** Sleep boosts your immune system, helping your body fend off infections and illnesses.
5. **Energy Conservation:** Sleep helps conserve energy, giving your body a chance to rest and prepare for the next day.

The Stages of Sleep

Sleep isn't a single, uniform state. It's made up of different stages, each with its own characteristics and functions. Let's break down these stages:

1. **NREM Stage 1 (N1):** This is the lightest stage of sleep, often described as the transition between wakefulness and sleep. You might experience muscle twitches and a sensation of falling.
2. **NREM Stage 2 (N2):** This stage is characterized by a slowing heart rate and a decrease in body temperature. It's a deeper sleep than N1, and it's harder to wake up from.

3. **NREM Stage 3 (N3):** Also known as deep sleep or slow-wave sleep, this stage is crucial for physical restoration. Your body repairs tissues, builds muscle, and strengthens the immune system.
4. **REM Sleep:** REM stands for Rapid Eye Movement. This stage is when most dreaming occurs. Your brain activity is similar to that of being awake, and it's essential for cognitive functions like memory and learning.

The Sleep Cycle

We don't just go through these stages once a night; instead, we cycle through them multiple times. A typical sleep cycle lasts about 90 minutes and repeats four to six times per night. Understanding this cycle can help you optimize your sleep patterns. For instance, if you wake up feeling groggy, it might be because your alarm went off during deep sleep. Timing your wake-up to coincide with lighter sleep stages can make mornings more pleasant.

The Importance of REM Sleep

REM sleep is particularly fascinating. During this stage, your brain is highly active, almost as if you're awake. Your eyes dart around rapidly, and this is when most dreaming occurs. REM sleep is essential for:

1. **Memory Consolidation:** Your brain processes and stores information from the day.
2. **Emotional Regulation:** REM sleep helps you manage and process emotions.
3. **Creativity:** Many people report increased creativity and problem-solving abilities after a good night's sleep.

The Impact of Sleep Deprivation

What happens when you don't get enough sleep? The effects of sleep deprivation can be severe and far-reaching:

1. **Cognitive Impairment:** Lack of sleep affects your ability to think clearly, concentrate, and make decisions.
2. **Emotional Instability:** You're more likely to experience mood swings, irritability, and stress.
3. **Physical Health Issues:** Chronic sleep deprivation is linked to serious health problems like heart disease, diabetes, and obesity.
4. **Weakened Immune System:** Your body's ability to fight off infections is compromised.
5. **Increased Risk of Accidents:** Sleep-deprived individuals are more prone to accidents and injuries.

Tips for Better Sleep

Now that we know how crucial sleep is, let's look at some practical tips to improve your sleep quality:

1. **Stick to a Schedule:** Go to bed and wake up at the same time every day, even on weekends. This helps regulate your body's internal clock.
2. **Create a Relaxing Bedtime Routine:** Engage in calming activities before bed, such as reading, taking a warm bath, or practicing relaxation techniques.

3. **Optimize Your Sleep Environment:** Make your bedroom a sleep haven. Keep it cool, dark, and quiet. Invest in a comfortable mattress and pillows.
4. **Limit Exposure to Screens:** The blue light emitted by phones, tablets, and computers can interfere with your sleep. Try to avoid screens at least an hour before bedtime.
5. **Watch Your Diet:** Avoid heavy meals, caffeine, and alcohol close to bedtime. Opt for light, sleep-friendly snacks if you're hungry.
6. **Stay Active:** Regular physical activity can help you fall asleep faster and enjoy deeper sleep. Just avoid vigorous exercise close to bedtime.
7. **Manage Stress:** Stress and anxiety can interfere with your ability to fall asleep. Practice stress management techniques like deep breathing, meditation, or journaling.

Understanding Sleep Disorders

Sometimes, despite our best efforts, sleep remains elusive. In such cases, a sleep disorder might be to blame. Here are some common sleep disorders and their symptoms:

1. **Insomnia:** Difficulty falling or staying asleep. This can be caused by stress, anxiety, depression, or other factors.
2. **Sleep Apnea:** A condition where breathing repeatedly stops and starts during sleep. Symptoms include loud snoring, choking, or gasping for air.

3. **Restless Legs Syndrome (RLS):** An uncomfortable sensation in the legs that creates an irresistible urge to move them.
4. **Narcolepsy:** A disorder characterized by excessive daytime sleepiness and sudden sleep attacks.

If you suspect you have a sleep disorder, it's essential to seek medical advice. Proper diagnosis and treatment can significantly improve your sleep quality and overall health.

The Role of Dreams

Dreams are one of the most intriguing aspects of sleep. While their exact purpose remains a mystery, scientists believe that dreams play a role in:

1. **Processing Emotions:** Dreams help you process and make sense of your emotions and experiences.
2. **Problem-Solving:** Sometimes, dreams can offer creative solutions to problems you face while awake.
3. **Memory Consolidation:** Dreams might help in organizing and storing memories.

The Future of Sleep Science

The study of sleep is an ever-evolving field. Researchers are continually uncovering new insights into how sleep affects our health and well-being. Future advancements might include personalized sleep treatments, better understanding of sleep disorders, and innovative technologies to enhance sleep quality.

Embracing the Power of Sleep

Sleep isn't just a passive activity; it's a powerful tool for enhancing your health, productivity, and overall quality of life. By understanding the science of sleep, you can take proactive steps to improve your sleep habits and enjoy the numerous benefits that come with a good night's rest.

So, next time you find yourself tempted to sacrifice sleep for work or entertainment, remember the incredible benefits of a well-rested mind and body. Embrace the power of sleep, and you'll be well on your way to transforming your mornings and achieving lifelong success.

Sweet dreams and happy mornings!

5 Silence—Finding Inner Peace

Hello, peace-seekers! Have you ever stopped to think about how noisy our world has become? From the constant buzz of notifications to the hum of daily activities, finding a moment of true silence can feel like discovering a hidden gem. Today, we're exploring "Silence – Finding Inner Peace," a vital component of transforming your mornings and, ultimately, your life. So, find a quiet spot, take a deep breath, and let's journey into the tranquil world of silence together.

The Power of Silence

Silence is often underrated in our fast-paced, noise-filled lives. Yet, it holds incredible power to heal, rejuvenate, and bring clarity. Here's why silence is so powerful:

1. **Mental Clarity:** Silence allows your mind to rest and recharge. It creates space for clear thinking and deeper understanding.
2. **Stress Reduction:** In the absence of noise, your body can relax, reducing stress hormones and promoting a sense of calm.
3. **Enhanced Creativity:** Without the constant barrage of external stimuli, your brain can wander and explore new ideas, boosting creativity.
4. **Emotional Balance:** Silence helps you tune into your inner world, allowing you to process emotions and find balance.
5. **Spiritual Connection:** Many people find that silence fosters a deeper connection with their spiritual selves, leading to greater inner peace.

Creating a Silent Space

To tap into the benefits of silence, it's essential to create a space where you can experience true quiet. Here are some tips to carve out your silent sanctuary:

1. **Choose the Right Time:** Early mornings or late evenings are often the quietest times of day. Choose a time when you're least likely to be disturbed.
2. **Designate a Quiet Area:** Find a spot in your home where you can sit comfortably without distractions. This could be a cozy corner, a favorite chair, or even a spot in your garden.
3. **Limit Noise Pollution:** Turn off electronic devices and, if needed, use earplugs or noise-canceling headphones to block out external noise.

4. **Set Boundaries:** Let family members or housemates know that you need some quiet time. Setting boundaries ensures you have uninterrupted silence.

5. **Natural Silence:** Spending time in nature can provide a profound sense of peace. A walk in the park or a hike in the woods offers natural silence that's deeply rejuvenating.

Embracing Silence in Your Morning Routine

Integrating silence into your morning routine can set a peaceful tone for the rest of your day. Here's how to incorporate moments of silence into your mornings:

1. **Silent Wake-Up:** Start your day without reaching for your phone or turning on the TV. Take a few moments to simply sit in silence and appreciate the new day.

2. **Mindful Meditation:** Spend 10-15 minutes in silent meditation. Focus on your breath, let go of thoughts, and embrace the stillness. This practice can center your mind and prepare you for the day ahead.

3. **Silent Walk:** If you enjoy morning walks, try doing them in silence. Pay attention to the sounds of nature, your footsteps, and your breath. This mindful practice can be incredibly grounding.

4. **Gratitude Reflection:** Sit quietly and reflect on things you're grateful for. This silent reflection can boost your mood and set a positive tone for the day.

5. **Journaling:** Spend a few minutes writing in your journal. The act of writing in silence can help you connect with your inner thoughts and feelings.

The Science Behind Silence

Believe it or not, there's scientific evidence to back up the benefits of silence. Here are some key findings:

1. **Brain Growth:** A study published in the journal *Brain, Structure, and Function* found that two hours of silence daily could lead to the development of new cells in the hippocampus, the brain region associated with memory and emotion.
2. **Stress Reduction:** Silence has been shown to lower blood pressure and reduce levels of cortisol, the stress hormone. This promotes overall well-being and heart health.
3. **Improved Focus:** Research indicates that silence can enhance cognitive functions, including improved focus, attention, and problem-solving abilities.
4. **Emotional Health:** Silence allows for self-reflection, helping individuals process emotions and experiences more effectively, leading to better emotional health.

Overcoming the Challenges of Silence

Embracing silence isn't always easy, especially in a world that values constant activity and noise. Here are some common challenges and how to overcome them:

1. **Restlessness:** If you're not used to silence, you might feel restless or uncomfortable. Start with short periods of silence and gradually increase the duration as you become more comfortable.
2. **Intrusive Thoughts:** It's normal for thoughts to arise during silence. Instead of fighting them,

acknowledge them and gently return your focus to your breath or the present moment.

3. **Distractions:** External distractions can disrupt your silent time. Create a calm environment and communicate your need for quiet to those around you.

4. **Guilt:** Some people feel guilty taking time for themselves. Remember, prioritizing your well-being isn't selfish; it's essential for a balanced, healthy life.

Real-Life Stories of Finding Inner Peace Through Silence

Hearing from others who've embraced silence can be inspiring. Here are a few real-life stories:

1. **Anna, Corporate Executive:** "I used to feel constantly stressed and overwhelmed. Incorporating silent meditation into my morning routine has been life-changing. It's my time to reset and find balance before a busy day."

2. **Michael, Artist:** "As an artist, I thrive on creativity. Spending time in silence allows my mind to wander and explore new ideas. It's in those quiet moments that I find my best inspiration."

3. **Lily, Stay-at-Home Mom:** "With kids, silence is rare. But I started waking up 30 minutes earlier to enjoy a cup of tea in silence. It's my moment of peace before the chaos of the day begins."

Practical Exercises to Cultivate Silence

Ready to bring more silence into your life? Here are some practical exercises to help you get started:

1. **Breath Awareness:** Sit comfortably and close your eyes. Focus on your breath, feeling the air enter and leave your body. When your mind wanders, gently bring it back to your breath.
2. **Body Scan:** Lie down and close your eyes. Slowly bring your attention to each part of your body, starting from your toes and moving up to your head. Notice any sensations without judgment.
3. **Nature Listening:** Find a quiet spot in nature. Sit and listen to the sounds around you—the rustling leaves, chirping birds, or flowing water. Let these natural sounds soothe your mind.
4. **Silent Retreats:** Consider attending a silent retreat, where you can immerse yourself in extended periods of silence. These retreats offer a deep divc into the practice of silence and inner peace.

The Long-Term Benefits of Silence

Incorporating silence into your daily routine offers long-term benefits that go beyond immediate relaxation. Here's what you can expect:

1. **Greater Self-Awareness:** Silence helps you connect with your inner self, leading to increased self-awareness and personal growth.
2. **Improved Relationships:** By finding peace within yourself, you're better equipped to maintain healthy and balanced relationships with others.
3. **Enhanced Productivity:** A clear, focused mind can tackle tasks more efficiently, boosting your productivity and effectiveness.
4. **Better Decision-Making:** Silence fosters deep thinking and reflection, leading to better decision-making and problem-solving skills.

Embracing Silence in a Noisy World

In today's world, finding silence can be a challenge, but it's worth the effort. Here are some tips for embracing silence amidst the noise:

1. **Digital Detox:** Take regular breaks from technology. Turn off notifications and set aside time each day to disconnect from screens.
2. **Quiet Time Rituals:** Establish daily rituals that incorporate silence, such as morning meditation, silent meals, or evening reflections.
3. **Mindful Commuting:** Use your commute as an opportunity for silence. Instead of listening to music or podcasts, embrace the quiet and observe your surroundings.
4. **Silent Activities:** Engage in activities that promote silence, such as gardening, drawing, or walking. These activities can be both calming and rejuvenating.

Your Journey to Inner Peace

Finding inner peace through silence is a journey, not a destination. It's about making small, intentional changes to your daily routine and embracing the quiet moments. As you cultivate silence, you'll discover a profound sense of tranquility and clarity that can transform your mornings and your life.

So, are you ready to embrace the power of silence? Start today by carving out a few minutes of quiet time and experience the peace and clarity it brings. Here's to finding inner peace and transforming your mornings into moments of pure serenity!

6

Affirmations—Rewiring Your Brain

Have you ever wished you could reprogram your brain to think more positively, achieve your goals, and live a more fulfilling life? Well, the good news is that you can! Today, we're diving into the fascinating world of affirmations and how they can help you rewire your brain for success. So, grab your favorite morning beverage, get comfortable, and let's explore how affirmations can transform your mornings and your life.

What Are Affirmations?

Affirmations are positive statements that you repeat to yourself regularly to challenge and overcome negative thoughts and self-doubt. They are like mental vitamins, providing a boost to your mindset and helping you build a more positive and confident outlook on life.

Think of affirmations as little messages of encouragement that you give yourself. They can be about anything you want to improve or achieve, from building self-esteem to reaching career goals. Here's why affirmations are so powerful:

1. **Positive Reinforcement:** Affirmations reinforce positive thoughts and beliefs, replacing negative self-talk with empowering messages.
2. **Focus on Goals:** By regularly repeating your goals and aspirations, affirmations help keep you focused and motivated.
3. **Mindset Shift:** Affirmations can shift your mindset from scarcity and limitation to abundance and possibility.

The Science Behind Affirmations

You might be wondering, do affirmations really work? The answer is yes, and there's science to back it up. Here's how affirmations can rewire your brain:

1. **Neuroplasticity:** Our brains are incredibly adaptable, thanks to a concept known as neuroplasticity. This means that the brain can form new neural connections and pathways in response to thoughts, behaviors, and experiences. Affirmations tap into this ability by creating positive neural pathways.
2. **Cognitive Dissonance:** When you repeat an affirmation, your brain experiences a conflict between your current belief and the new positive statement. To resolve this, your brain starts aligning your thoughts and behaviors

with the affirmation, gradually changing your mindset.

3. **Self-Affirmation Theory:** According to this psychological theory, affirmations help maintain our self-identity by reinforcing our values and beliefs. This boosts our self-worth and confidence.

Crafting Effective Affirmations

Not all affirmations are created equal. To harness the full power of affirmations, it's essential to craft them effectively. Here are some tips:

1. **Be Positive:** Focus on what you want, not what you don't want. Instead of saying, "I am not stressed," say, "I am calm and relaxed."
2. **Be Specific:** General affirmations can be less effective. Be specific about what you want to achieve. For example, "I am a successful writer" is more powerful than "I am successful."
3. **Use Present Tense:** Phrase your affirmations as if they are already true. This helps your brain start believing them. For example, "I am confident" rather than "I will be confident."
4. **Keep It Simple:** Short, simple affirmations are easier to remember and repeat. They should be clear and concise.
5. **Make It Personal:** Your affirmations should resonate with you personally. Use words and phrases that feel meaningful and authentic to you.

Incorporating Affirmations Into Your Morning Routine

Morning is a perfect time to practice affirmations. Starting your day with positive statements sets the tone for the rest of the day. Here's how to seamlessly incorporate affirmations into your morning routine:

1. **Morning Mirror:** Stand in front of a mirror and repeat your affirmations aloud. Looking at yourself while saying positive statements can enhance their impact.
2. **Affirmation Journal:** Keep a journal where you write down your affirmations each morning. This practice reinforces your commitment and helps you reflect on your progress.
3. **Mindful Meditation:** Incorporate affirmations into your morning meditation. As you meditate, repeat your affirmations silently or aloud, focusing on the positive feelings they evoke.
4. **Affirmation Cards:** Write your affirmations on small cards and place them where you'll see them throughout the morning—on your bathroom mirror, fridge, or desk.
5. **Digital Reminders:** Set up digital reminders on your phone or computer to prompt you with your affirmations at specific times each morning.

Real-Life Affirmation Success Stories

Hearing about how others have benefited from affirmations can be incredibly inspiring. Here are a few real-life stories:

1. **Sarah, Entrepreneur:** "Starting my day with affirmations has transformed my business mindset. I used to doubt my abilities, but now I confidently say, 'I am a successful entrepreneur, and my business thrives.' It's amazing how this simple practice has boosted my confidence and performance."
2. **John, Athlete:** "Affirmations have helped me push through tough training sessions and competitions. Every morning, I tell myself, 'I am strong, focused, and capable of achieving my goals.' It keeps me motivated and resilient."
3. **Emily, Student:** "As a student, I often felt overwhelmed. I started using affirmations like 'I am intelligent and capable of learning anything.' It's made a huge difference in my confidence and academic performance."

Overcoming Challenges with Affirmations

While affirmations are powerful, they can sometimes feel awkward or ineffective, especially when you're just starting out. Here's how to overcome common challenges:

1. **Feeling Silly:** It's normal to feel a bit silly when you first start saying affirmations. Remember, this is a personal practice, and the more you do it, the more natural it will feel.
2. **Doubt:** If you don't believe your affirmations at first, that's okay. Consistency is key. Over time, repeating affirmations will help shift your beliefs.
3. **Impatience:** Affirmations aren't a quick fix. It takes time for your brain to rewire and for

you to notice changes. Be patient and persistent.

4. **Finding Time:** Incorporate affirmations into your existing routine to make them a habit. Whether it's during your morning coffee or while brushing your teeth, find a consistent time that works for you.

Affirmations for Different Aspects of Life

Affirmations can be tailored to various areas of your life. Here are some examples:

1. **Self-Esteem:** "I am worthy of love and respect." "I believe in myself and my abilities."
2. **Health:** "I am healthy, strong, and full of energy." "I make choices that support my well-being."
3. **Career:** "I am successful in my career." "I attract opportunities that align with my goals."
4. **Relationships:** "I deserve loving and supportive relationships." "I communicate effectively and with kindness."
5. **Stress Management:** "I am calm and centered." "I handle challenges with grace and ease."

The Long-Term Benefits of Affirmations

Consistently practicing affirmations can lead to profound long-term benefits:

1. **Increased Confidence:** Repeating positive statements about yourself builds self-confidence and self-worth.
2. **Improved Mental Health:** Affirmations can reduce negative thoughts and stress,

promoting better mental health.

3. **Enhanced Focus:** By focusing on your goals and positive beliefs, affirmations help improve your focus and determination.
4. **Greater Resilience:** Affirmations build mental strength, helping you bounce back from setbacks more effectively.
5. **Positive Relationships:** As you cultivate a positive mindset, you'll find that your relationships improve as well. Positivity is contagious!

Your Affirmation Journey

Starting an affirmation practice is a journey, and like any journey, it requires commitment and persistence. Here are some steps to get you started:

1. **Identify Your Goals:** What do you want to achieve or improve in your life? Your affirmations should align with these goals.
2. **Create Your Affirmations:** Use the tips we've discussed to craft effective affirmations. Write them down and keep them handy.
3. **Repeat Daily:** Consistency is key. Repeat your affirmations daily, preferably in the morning to set a positive tone for the day.
4. **Reflect and Adjust:** Periodically reflect on your affirmations and their impact. Adjust them as needed to ensure they remain relevant and effective.
5. **Celebrate Progress:** Acknowledge and celebrate the positive changes you notice. This reinforces your practice and keeps you motivated.

Unfuck Your Morning with Affirmations

Affirmations are a powerful tool for rewiring your brain and transforming your life. By incorporating them into your morning routine, you can start each day with positivity, focus, and confidence. Remember, the journey to change begins with a single step—or in this case, a single positive statement.

Embrace the power of positive thinking and watch as your life begins to align with your dreams and goals. Here's to a brighter, more empowered you!

7 Visualization—Creating Your Desired Reality

Hello, dream builders! Have you ever heard the saying, "If you can dream it, you can do it"? Visualization is the powerful technique behind this idea, and it's something anyone can learn to harness. Today, we're diving into the fascinating world of visualization—how you can use this tool to create your desired reality and transform your mornings into a launchpad for lifelong success. So, grab a comfy spot, take a deep breath, and let's explore how to turn your dreams into reality through the power of visualization.

What Is Visualization?

Visualization is a mental technique that involves creating vivid images in your mind of what you want to achieve or experience. It's like daydreaming with a purpose. When you visualize, you use your imagination to picture your goals as if they've already been accomplished, engaging all your senses to make the experience as real as possible.

Think of visualization as a mental rehearsal. Athletes use it to improve performance, business professionals use it to achieve goals, and anyone can use it to manifest their desires. Here's why visualization is so effective:

1. **Mental Blueprint:** Visualization creates a mental blueprint of what you want to achieve, helping your brain recognize opportunities to make it happen.
2. **Emotional Engagement:** By vividly imagining your success, you engage your emotions, which can boost motivation and persistence.
3. **Mind-Body Connection:** Visualization can improve physical performance by mentally rehearsing actions, creating neural pathways that enhance actual performance.

The Science Behind Visualization

You might be wondering, does visualization really work? The answer is a resounding yes, and there's science to back it up:

1. **Neuroplasticity:** Our brains are incredibly adaptable, thanks to a concept called neuroplasticity. Visualization helps form new neural connections, making your brain more receptive to achieving your goals.
2. **Mirror Neurons:** When you visualize an action, your brain activates the same neural

pathways as if you were actually performing the action. This primes your brain for success.

3. **Stress Reduction:** Visualization can reduce stress by creating a mental escape and promoting relaxation, which in turn enhances performance and well-being.

How to Practice Visualization

Ready to start visualizing your dreams into reality? Here's a step-by-step guide to effective visualization:

1. **Find a Quiet Space:** Choose a quiet, comfortable place where you won't be disturbed. This helps you focus fully on your visualization practice.
2. **Relax Your Body:** Take a few deep breaths and relax your body. Close your eyes and let go of any tension. A calm, relaxed state is ideal for visualization.
3. **Set a Clear Intention:** Know exactly what you want to visualize. Whether it's a career goal, a personal achievement, or a desired experience, be specific.
4. **Engage All Senses:** Make your visualization as vivid as possible. Imagine the sights, sounds, smells, tastes, and physical sensations associated with your desired reality.
5. **Emotionally Connect:** Feel the emotions of achieving your goal. Whether it's joy, pride, or excitement, emotional engagement makes your visualization more powerful.
6. **Practice Regularly:** Consistency is key. Practice visualization daily, preferably in the morning to set a positive tone for the day.

Incorporating Visualization into Your Morning Routine

Mornings are an excellent time for visualization. Starting your day by mentally rehearsing your goals can set a positive, focused tone for the rest of the day. Here's how to seamlessly integrate visualization into your morning routine:

1. **Morning Meditation:** Combine visualization with your morning meditation. After a few minutes of calming your mind, spend five minutes visualizing your desired reality.
2. **Visualization Journal:** Keep a journal where you write down your visualizations. Describe your goals in detail, including the sensory and emotional aspects. Reviewing your journal each morning reinforces your practice.
3. **Vision Board:** Create a vision board with images and words that represent your goals. Spend a few minutes each morning looking at your vision board and visualizing your success.
4. **Affirmations and Visualization:** Pair your visualizations with positive affirmations. As you visualize, repeat affirmations that align with your goals to strengthen your belief in your desired reality.
5. **Mindful Visualization Walk:** Take a short walk in the morning and use that time to visualize your goals. Walking can help you relax and focus, making your visualizations more vivid and effective.

Overcoming Common Challenges

While visualization is powerful, you might face some challenges when starting out. Here's how to overcome them:

1. **Difficulty Concentrating:** If you find it hard to concentrate, start with short visualization sessions and gradually increase the duration as your focus improves.
2. **Negative Thoughts:** It's normal for negative thoughts to arise. When they do, gently redirect your focus to your positive visualization. Over time, this will become easier.
3. **Impatience:** Visualization isn't a quick fix. It takes time and consistency to see results. Be patient and persistent, and trust the process.
4. **Lack of Clarity:** If you're unsure about your goals, spend some time reflecting on what you truly want. Clarity will make your visualizations more effective.

Visualization for Different Aspects of Life

Visualization can be applied to various areas of your life. Here are some examples:

1. **Career Success:** Visualize yourself thriving in your career. See yourself achieving your goals, receiving recognition, and enjoying your work.
2. **Health and Fitness:** Picture yourself in optimal health and fitness. Imagine yourself feeling strong, energetic, and full of vitality.
3. **Relationships:** Visualize positive, loving

relationships. See yourself connecting deeply with others and enjoying fulfilling interactions.

4. **Personal Growth:** Imagine yourself growing and evolving. Visualize yourself learning new skills, overcoming challenges, and becoming the best version of yourself.
5. **Financial Abundance:** Picture yourself enjoying financial abundance. See yourself managing your finances wisely, achieving financial goals, and experiencing prosperity.

The Long-Term Benefits of Visualization

Consistent visualization practice can lead to profound long-term benefits:

1. **Increased Confidence:** Visualization builds confidence by mentally rehearsing success and reinforcing positive self-beliefs.
2. **Enhanced Focus:** By regularly visualizing your goals, you keep them at the forefront of your mind, improving your focus and determination.
3. **Improved Performance:** Visualization enhances performance by creating neural pathways that support actual skill development and execution.
4. **Greater Resilience:** Visualization helps you mentally prepare for challenges, making you more resilient and adaptable.
5. **Manifestation of Goals:** Over time, visualization can help manifest your goals and desires into reality by aligning your thoughts, emotions, and actions.

Your Visualization Journey

Embarking on a visualization journey is a powerful step toward creating your desired reality. Here are some steps to get you started:

1. **Set Clear Goals:** Identify what you want to achieve or experience. Your visualizations should be specific and meaningful to you.
2. **Create Detailed Visualizations:** Make your visualizations vivid and engaging by incorporating sensory details and emotions.
3. **Practice Daily:** Consistency is key. Set aside time each morning for your visualization practice.
4. **Reflect and Adjust:** Periodically reflect on your visualizations and their impact. Adjust them as needed to ensure they remain relevant and effective.
5. **Celebrate Progress:** Acknowledge and celebrate the positive changes you notice. This reinforces your practice and keeps you motivated.

Shine with Visualization

Visualization is a powerful tool for creating your desired reality and transforming your life. By incorporating this practice into your morning routine, you can start each day with clarity, focus, and inspiration. Remember, the journey to achieving your dreams begins in your mind.

Embrace the power of your imagination and watch as your dreams take shape and become your reality. Here's to a brighter, more fulfilling future!

8 Exercise—Energizing Your Body

Hello, movers and shakers! Are you ready to start your day feeling vibrant, energized, and ready to take on the world? If so, it's time to embrace the power of morning exercise. Today, we're exploring how exercise can energize your body, boost your mood, and set you up for a day of success and productivity. So, lace up your shoes, get pumped, and let's dive into the world of morning exercise!

Why Exercise in the Morning?

You might be wondering, why should I exercise in the morning when I could do it later in the day? Here are some compelling reasons to make morning exercise a part of your routine:

1. **Boosted Energy Levels:** Starting your day with physical activity increases your energy levels and helps you feel more awake and alert.
2. **Enhanced Mood:** Exercise releases endorphins, the "feel-good" hormones, which can improve your mood and set a positive tone for the day.
3. **Increased Productivity:** Physical activity can enhance cognitive function, helping you stay focused and productive throughout the day.
4. **Better Sleep:** Morning exercise can help regulate your sleep patterns, leading to better sleep quality and more restful nights.
5. **Consistent Routine:** Exercising in the morning ensures that you get your workout done before the day's demands can interfere.

The Science Behind Morning Exercise

Exercise isn't just good for your body; it's great for your brain too. Here's how morning exercise impacts your physiology and mental state:

1. **Improved Cardiovascular Health:** Regular exercise strengthens your heart and improves blood circulation, reducing the risk of cardiovascular diseases.
2. **Enhanced Brain Function:** Exercise increases blood flow to the brain, promoting the growth of new neurons and enhancing cognitive functions like memory and learning.
3. **Stress Reduction:** Physical activity reduces levels of the stress hormone cortisol, helping you feel more relaxed and less anxious.
4. **Hormonal Balance:** Exercise helps regulate hormones that influence mood, energy levels,

and appetite, contributing to overall well-being.

Creating a Morning Exercise Routine

Ready to make morning exercise a habit? Here's how to create a routine that works for you:

1. **Start Small:** If you're new to morning exercise, start with short, manageable workouts. Even 10-15 minutes can make a big difference.
2. **Choose Enjoyable Activities:** Find exercises that you enjoy, whether it's running, yoga, dancing, or strength training. Enjoyment increases the likelihood of sticking with your routine.
3. **Prepare the Night Before:** Lay out your workout clothes and equipment the night before. This makes it easier to get started in the morning.
4. **Set a Consistent Time:** Choose a specific time for your morning workout and stick to it. Consistency helps establish a habit.
5. **Warm-Up and Cool Down:** Begin with a warm-up to prepare your body and end with a cool-down to aid recovery. This reduces the risk of injury and improves performance.

Types of Morning Workouts

There are countless ways to get moving in the morning. Here are some types of workouts to consider:

1. **Cardio Workouts:** Activities like running, cycling, or jumping rope elevate your heart rate and improve cardiovascular health. Aim for 20-30 minutes to start your day with a burst of energy.

2. **Strength Training:** Incorporate bodyweight exercises like push-ups, squats, and planks, or use weights to build muscle and increase metabolism.
3. **Yoga and Stretching:** Yoga combines physical activity with mindfulness, helping you build strength, flexibility, and mental clarity. Stretching can also improve flexibility and reduce muscle tension.
4. **High-Intensity Interval Training (HIIT):** HIIT workouts involve short bursts of intense activity followed by rest periods. These workouts are efficient and effective for boosting fitness and burning calories.
5. **Dance Workouts:** Dancing is a fun way to get your heart rate up and improve coordination. Plus, it's a great mood booster!

Overcoming Common Challenges

Starting a morning exercise routine can be challenging. Here's how to overcome common obstacles:

1. **Difficulty Waking Up:** If you struggle to get out of bed, set your alarm 15 minutes earlier each day until you reach your desired wake-up time. Placing your alarm across the room can also help.
2. **Lack of Time:** If your mornings are rushed, prioritize short, high-intensity workouts that fit into your schedule. Even a quick 10-minute workout is better than none.
3. **Low Motivation:** Keep your workouts varied and enjoyable to maintain motivation. Consider finding a workout buddy or joining a fitness class for added accountability.

4. **Physical Discomfort:** Listen to your body and choose exercises that suit your fitness level. Gradually increase the intensity to avoid injury.

Tips for Staying Motivated

Staying motivated is key to maintaining a morning exercise routine. Here are some tips to keep you on track:

1. **Set Clear Goals:** Define what you want to achieve with your morning workouts. Whether it's improving fitness, boosting energy, or reducing stress, having clear goals keeps you motivated.
2. **Track Your Progress:** Keep a workout journal or use a fitness app to track your progress. Seeing your improvements over time can be highly motivating.
3. **Reward Yourself:** Set up a reward system for sticking to your routine. Treat yourself to something you enjoy, like a relaxing bath or a healthy snack.
4. **Mix It Up:** Vary your workouts to keep things interesting. Try new activities, change your workout location, or join a fitness class to keep your routine fresh.
5. **Visualize Success:** Spend a few moments each day visualizing the benefits of your morning workouts. Picture yourself feeling energized, strong, and ready to tackle the day.

The Long-Term Benefits of Morning Exercise

Consistent morning exercise offers long-term benefits that go beyond immediate physical fitness:

1. **Sustained Energy Levels:** Regular exercise boosts your overall energy levels, making you feel more vibrant and alive throughout the day.
2. **Improved Mental Health:** Physical activity reduces symptoms of anxiety and depression, promoting better mental health and emotional well-being.
3. **Enhanced Cognitive Function:** Exercise improves brain function, memory, and learning, helping you stay sharp and focused.
4. **Better Physical Health:** Regular exercise reduces the risk of chronic diseases like heart disease, diabetes, and obesity, contributing to a longer, healthier life.
5. **Positive Lifestyle Changes:** Establishing a morning exercise routine can inspire other healthy habits, such as better nutrition and sleep hygiene.

Your Morning Exercise Journey

Starting a morning exercise routine is a journey that requires commitment and perseverance. Here are some steps to help you get started and stay on track:

1. **Set Realistic Goals:** Begin with achievable goals that suit your fitness level and lifestyle. Gradually increase the intensity and duration of your workouts as you progress.
2. **Find What You Love:** Experiment with different types of exercise to find what you enjoy most. When you love what you're doing, it's easier to stick with it.
3. **Create a Support System:** Share your goals with friends or family members who can

support and encourage you. Consider finding a workout buddy for added accountability.

4. **Listen to Your Body:** Pay attention to how your body responds to exercise. Rest when needed and avoid pushing yourself too hard.
5. **Celebrate Milestones:** Celebrate your achievements, no matter how small. Each step forward is a victory on your journey to a healthier, more energized life.

Unfuck Your Morning with Morning Exercise

Morning exercise is a powerful way to energize your body, boost your mood, and set a positive tone for the day. By incorporating physical activity into your morning routine, you can transform your mornings and achieve lifelong success.

Embrace the energy, vitality, and joy that comes from moving your body and taking care of your health. Here's to a brighter, more vibrant you!

9 Reading—Expanding Your Mind

Have you ever felt the thrill of diving into a good book, losing track of time as you explore new worlds, ideas, and perspectives? Reading is not just a pastime; it's a powerful tool for expanding your mind and transforming your mornings into moments of growth and inspiration. Today, we're going to explore how reading can enrich your life, boost your mental faculties, and set you on a path to lifelong success. So, grab your favorite book, settle in, and let's embark on this literary journey together!

The Power of Reading

Reading is like a magic key that unlocks the doors to countless worlds and experiences. Here's why reading is so powerful:

1. **Knowledge Acquisition:** Books are treasure troves of information. Whether you're reading fiction or non-fiction, every page offers new insights and knowledge.
2. **Mental Stimulation:** Reading stimulates your brain, improving cognitive functions like memory, focus, and critical thinking.
3. **Stress Reduction:** Getting lost in a good book can be a great escape from the stresses of daily life, providing a mental break and relaxation.
4. **Empathy and Understanding:** Through reading, you can walk in someone else's shoes, gaining empathy and a deeper understanding of different cultures, perspectives, and experiences.
5. **Vocabulary Expansion:** Regular reading exposes you to new words and phrases, enhancing your language skills and communication abilities.

Incorporating Reading into Your Morning Routine

Mornings are a powerful time for personal growth, and incorporating reading into your morning ritual can set the tone for an inspired, focused day. This habit not only expands your knowledge but also primes your mind for success.

1. **Start Small:** Begin with just 10–15 minutes of reading in the morning. A short, intentional session ensures the habit feels manageable and doesn't overwhelm your schedule. Over time, you can increase the duration.
2. **Choose Your Content Wisely:** What you read in the morning can influence your mindset for the

entire day. Opt for uplifting, motivational, or educational material. Books on self-improvement, biographies of inspiring figures, or thought-provoking articles are excellent choices.

3. **Pair Reading with Other Habits:** Stack your reading habit onto an existing morning routine. For example, read while sipping your coffee, journaling, or during your meditation cooldown. This creates a seamless flow and eliminates resistance.
4. **Set a Goal:** Having a reading goal provides direction. This could be finishing one chapter, reading a set number of pages, or learning one new concept each day. Small achievements compound over time and keep you motivated.
5. **Go Analog in the Morning:** Avoid starting your day with screens. Opt for physical books or a Kindle with minimal distractions. Digital reading often leads to mindless scrolling, derailing the focus you need in the morning.
6. **Reflect on What You Read:** Dedicate a minute or two after reading to reflect on how the material resonates with you. Write down key takeaways or a single idea that can guide your day. This simple step solidifies what you've learned and encourages application.

By making reading a staple in your morning routine, you prime your brain for creativity, wisdom, and growth. It's not just about expanding your mind but also about creating a ripple effect of positivity that carries you through the day.

Benefits of Reading in the Morning

Incorporating reading into your morning routine offers numerous benefits that extend throughout the day. Here are some ways reading in the morning can enhance your life:

1. **Mental Alertness:** Reading stimulates your brain and helps wake up your mind, making you more alert and focused for the rest of the day.
2. **Positive Mindset:** Starting your day with inspirational or motivational material can set a positive tone and boost your mood.
3. **Enhanced Creativity:** Exposure to new ideas and perspectives can spark your creativity and inspire innovative thinking.
4. **Stress Reduction:** A few minutes of reading in the morning can help reduce stress and create a calm, centered mindset.
5. **Lifelong Learning:** Regular reading fosters a habit of continuous learning, keeping your mind sharp and curious.

Real-Life Success Stories

Many successful individuals attribute part of their success to their reading habits. Here are a few inspiring examples:

1. **Bill Gates:** The co-founder of Microsoft is an avid reader and credits much of his success to the knowledge and insights he gains from books. He even shares book recommendations and reviews on his blog, GatesNotes.
2. **Oprah Winfrey:** Oprah has often spoken about how reading has transformed her life. Her book club has inspired millions to read and discuss literature, and she believes that reading is a key to personal growth.
3. **Elon Musk:** The CEO of SpaceX and Tesla has said that he learned how to build rockets

by reading books. Musk's voracious reading habit has been a significant factor in his ability to innovate and succeed in multiple industries.

Tips for Staying Consistent

Starting a morning reading routine is one thing; staying consistent is another. Here are some tips to help you maintain this beneficial habit:

1. **Set Achievable Goals:** Start with small, manageable goals. For example, aim to read for 10-15 minutes each morning and gradually increase the time as it becomes a habit.
2. **Track Your Progress:** Keep a reading log or use a reading app to track your progress. Seeing your progress can be motivating and help you stay committed.
3. **Join a Reading Group:** Joining a book club or reading group can provide accountability and make reading more social and enjoyable.
4. **Reward Yourself:** Treat yourself to something enjoyable after completing a book or reaching a reading milestone. Rewards can reinforce your commitment to the habit.
5. **Be Flexible:** Life can be unpredictable, so be flexible with your reading routine. If you miss a morning, don't get discouraged. Simply pick up where you left off the next day.

Creating a Reading-Friendly Environment

A conducive environment can enhance your reading experience and make it easier to stick to your routine. Here are some tips for creating a reading-friendly space:

1. **Comfortable Seating:** Choose a chair or spot that is comfortable and supports good posture. A cozy armchair or a cushion by the window can be inviting.
2. **Good Lighting:** Ensure you have adequate lighting for reading. Natural light is ideal, but a good reading lamp can also work wonders.
3. **Minimal Distractions:** Find a quiet spot where you can read without interruptions. Turn off notifications on your phone and create a peaceful atmosphere.
4. **Accessible Books:** Keep your current reads and a selection of books within easy reach. Having a variety of options can keep your reading habit fresh and exciting.
5. **Personal Touches:** Add personal touches to your reading nook, such as a favorite blanket, a scented candle, or a plant. These elements can make your reading time more enjoyable.

Rise and Shine with Reading

Reading is a powerful tool for expanding your mind and transforming your mornings. By incorporating this enriching habit into your daily routine, you can unlock new worlds of knowledge, inspiration, and personal growth. Whether you're diving into a novel, exploring a biography, or learning from a self-help book, reading can set the stage for a day of success and fulfillment.

So, rise and shine with reading! Embrace the magic of books and let them guide you on a journey of lifelong learning and discovery. Here's to a brighter, more informed, and inspired you!

10 Nutrition—Fueling the Day

Ever wonder why they say breakfast is the most important meal of the day? It's not just a saying—starting your day with the right nutrition can set you up for success, giving you the energy, focus, and vitality to tackle whatever comes your way. Today, we're diving into the topic of "Nutrition – Fueling the Day," exploring how to power up your mornings with delicious and nutritious foods. So grab your favorite morning beverage, and let's embark on this tasty journey together!

Why Morning Nutrition Matters

First things first, let's talk about why what you eat in the morning is so crucial. After a night of sleep, your body is in a fasted state. Breakfast, literally meaning "breaking the fast," replenishes your glucose supply, boosts your energy levels, and provides essential nutrients needed for good health. Here's why morning nutrition matters:

1. **Energy Boost:** A nutritious breakfast fuels your body, providing the energy needed to kickstart your day.
2. **Enhanced Focus:** Eating a balanced breakfast improves concentration and cognitive function, helping you stay alert and focused.
3. **Better Mood:** Certain foods can boost your mood and help reduce stress, setting a positive tone for the day.
4. **Metabolism Kickstart:** A healthy breakfast jumpstarts your metabolism, helping you burn calories more efficiently throughout the day.
5. **Long-Term Health:** Regularly eating a nutritious breakfast can help maintain a healthy weight, reduce the risk of chronic diseases, and support overall well-being.

Components of a Balanced Breakfast

So, what makes a breakfast truly nutritious and balanced? Here are the key components you should include:

1. **Complex Carbohydrates:** Provide sustained energy. Think whole grains like oats, whole wheat bread, and quinoa.
2. **Protein:** Keeps you full and supports muscle repair. Eggs, Greek yogurt, lean meats, and plant-based proteins like tofu are great options.

3. **Healthy Fats:** Essential for brain function and satiety. Include sources like avocados, nuts, seeds, and olive oil.
4. **Fiber:** Aids digestion and keeps you feeling full. Fruits, vegetables, and whole grains are excellent sources.
5. **Vitamins and Minerals:** Essential for various bodily functions. Aim to include a variety of fruits and vegetables to cover your bases.

Overcoming Common Breakfast Challenges

Sometimes, the morning rush can make it challenging to prioritize a healthy breakfast. Here's how to overcome common obstacles:

1. **Time Constraints:** If mornings are hectic, opt for quick and easy options like smoothies, yogurt parfaits, or overnight oats that you can grab and go.
2. **Lack of Appetite:** If you're not hungry in the morning, start with something light like a piece of fruit or a small smoothie. Gradually build up to more substantial meals as your body adjusts.
3. **Dietary Restrictions:** Whether you're gluten-free, dairy-free, or following another dietary plan, there are plenty of breakfast options available. Explore alternatives and get creative with your ingredients.
4. **Boredom:** Eating the same thing every day can get boring. Mix things up by trying new recipes or adding different toppings and flavors to your breakfast staples.

The Long-Term Benefits of a Nutritious Breakfast

Incorporating a healthy breakfast into your morning routine offers long-term benefits that go beyond immediate energy boosts:

1. **Weight Management:** Regularly eating a balanced breakfast can help regulate your appetite and prevent overeating later in the day, supporting healthy weight management.
2. **Improved Digestion:** A breakfast rich in fiber supports healthy digestion and prevents constipation.
3. **Better Blood Sugar Control:** Eating a balanced breakfast helps maintain stable blood sugar levels, reducing the risk of diabetes and other metabolic disorders.
4. **Enhanced Immune Function:** Nutrient-rich breakfasts support a healthy immune system, helping you fend off illnesses and infections.
5. **Sustained Energy Levels:** Starting your day with a nutritious meal ensures you have the energy to stay active and productive throughout the day.

Making Breakfast a Family Affair

Encouraging your family to join in on healthy breakfast habits can be a fun and bonding experience. Here are some tips for making breakfast a family affair:

1. **Get Everyone Involved:** Let family members choose their favorite breakfast options and involve them in the preparation process.

2. **Try New Recipes Together:** Explore new breakfast recipes as a family and make cooking breakfast a fun activity.
3. **Create a Breakfast Schedule:** Plan your weekly breakfasts together, ensuring a variety of options that everyone enjoys.
4. **Make It Enjoyable:** Set the table nicely, play some music, and create a pleasant breakfast atmosphere that everyone looks forward to.
5. **Lead by Example:** Demonstrate the importance of a nutritious breakfast by making it a priority for yourself. Your family is more likely to follow suit when they see you enjoying and benefiting from a healthy morning meal.

Fuel Your Morning with Nutrition

A nutritious breakfast is the foundation for a successful day. By fueling your body with the right foods, you set yourself up for sustained energy, improved focus, and better overall health. Embrace the power of morning nutrition and transform your mornings into moments of nourishment and vitality.

Make every morning an opportunity to fuel your body and mind, and watch as you unlock new levels of energy and success. Here's to a healthier, happier you, one delicious breakfast at a time!

11 Digital Detox—Starting Your Day Without Screens

Are you also a digital explorer! Have you ever wondered what it would be like to start your day without immediately diving into your phone, computer, or TV? In today's hyper-connected world, it's easy to feel tethered to our screens from the moment we wake up. But what if I told you that starting your day with a digital detox can lead to greater clarity, peace, and productivity? Today, we're exploring the transformative power of a morning digital detox and how it can set you on the path to lifelong success. So, put your devices on silent, take a deep breath, and let's discover the magic of screen-free mornings together.

Why a Digital Detox?

Let's start with the basics: why should you consider a digital detox, especially in the morning? Here are some compelling reasons:

1. **Mental Clarity:** Starting your day without screens allows your mind to wake up gradually and naturally, leading to greater mental clarity and focus.
2. **Reduced Stress:** Constant notifications and information overload can increase stress levels. A screen-free morning helps reduce this stress and promotes a sense of calm.
3. **Improved Mood:** Avoiding negative news or stressful emails first thing in the morning can help you maintain a positive mindset throughout the day.
4. **Enhanced Productivity:** Without the distraction of screens, you can focus on important tasks and set a productive tone for the rest of the day.
5. **Better Relationships:** A screen-free morning allows for more meaningful interactions with loved ones, fostering stronger relationships.

The Science Behind Digital Detox

The benefits of a digital detox are supported by science. Here's how unplugging can positively impact your brain and overall well-being:

1. **Reduced Cognitive Load:** Constant exposure to digital information can overload your brain, leading to fatigue and reduced cognitive function. A digital detox helps lighten this cognitive load.

2. **Improved Sleep Quality:** Blue light from screens can interfere with your sleep patterns. Avoiding screens in the morning and before bed can improve sleep quality.
3. **Enhanced Creativity:** Without the constant input from screens, your brain has more space for creative thinking and problem-solving.
4. **Lower Cortisol Levels:** Reducing screen time, especially in the morning, can lower cortisol levels (the stress hormone), promoting a more relaxed state.

How to Implement a Morning Digital Detox

Ready to give your mornings a digital detox? Here are some practical steps to help you get started:

1. **Set a Time Frame:** Decide how long you want to go without screens each morning. Start with 30 minutes and gradually increase the duration as you get used to it.
2. **Create a Morning Routine:** Develop a morning routine that doesn't involve screens. This could include activities like reading, journaling, exercising, or meditating.
3. **Use an Analog Alarm Clock:** Instead of using your phone as an alarm, opt for an analog alarm clock. This helps you avoid the temptation to check your phone first thing in the morning.
4. **Designate Screen-Free Zones:** Create specific areas in your home where screens are not allowed, such as the bedroom or dining room. This encourages more mindful use of technology.

5. **Plan Screen-Free Activities:** Have a list of enjoyable, screen-free activities ready for the morning. This could include hobbies, outdoor activities, or spending time with family.

Screen-Free Morning Activities

What can you do during your screen-free mornings? Here are some engaging and fulfilling activities to try:

1. **Mindful Meditation:** Start your day with a few minutes of meditation. Focus on your breath and set positive intentions for the day.
2. **Physical Exercise:** Engage in a morning workout, whether it's yoga, running, or a simple stretching routine. Exercise boosts energy and mood.
3. **Reading:** Enjoy a good book or read an inspiring article. Choose material that uplifts and motivates you.
4. **Journaling:** Write down your thoughts, goals, and gratitude. Journaling helps clear your mind and set a positive tone for the day.
5. **Outdoor Time:** Spend time in nature. Take a walk, enjoy your morning coffee on the porch, or simply sit and appreciate the beauty around you.
6. **Creative Pursuits:** Engage in a creative activity like drawing, painting, or playing a musical instrument. Creativity stimulates the brain and enhances well-being.
7. **Quality Time with Loved Ones:** Use the screen-free time to connect with family or friends. Have a meaningful conversation, play a game, or enjoy breakfast together.

Overcoming Challenges

Starting a morning digital detox can be challenging, especially if you're used to being constantly connected. Here are some tips to help you overcome common obstacles:

1. **Gradual Adjustment:** If the idea of a complete digital detox feels overwhelming, start small. Gradually increase your screen-free time each morning.
2. **Set Boundaries:** Communicate your digital detox plans with family and friends. Let them know you'll be unavailable during certain hours and stick to your boundaries.
3. **Replace Habits:** Identify the screen-based habits you want to change and replace them with healthier alternatives. For example, instead of scrolling through social media, read a book.
4. **Accountability:** Find a detox buddy or join a group of like-minded individuals who also want to reduce their screen time. Share your progress and support each other.
5. **Remind Yourself of the Benefits:** Keep a list of the benefits you're experiencing from your digital detox. Reflect on these positives whenever you feel tempted to check your phone.

Real-Life Success Stories

Hearing from others who have successfully implemented a morning digital detox can be inspiring. Here are a few real-life stories:

1. **Alex, Entrepreneur:** "Starting my day without screens has been a game-changer. I used to

feel overwhelmed by emails and notifications first thing in the morning. Now, I spend the first hour of my day exercising and journaling, and it's made me more focused and productive."

2. **Samantha, Teacher:** "I decided to try a morning digital detox after realizing how much time I was wasting on my phone. I now spend my mornings reading and meditating. I feel more centered and ready to face the day."
3. **Mark, Stay-at-Home Dad:** "With young kids, I wanted to be more present in the mornings. I stopped using my phone as an alarm and started my day with a walk outside. It's been great for my mental health and my relationship with my kids."

Long-Term Benefits of a Digital Detox

Incorporating a digital detox into your morning routine offers long-term benefits that can enhance your overall quality of life:

1. **Improved Mental Health:** Reduced screen time can lower stress levels and improve mood, contributing to better mental health.
2. **Enhanced Focus:** A screen-free morning helps improve concentration and cognitive function, making you more productive and efficient.
3. **Better Sleep Patterns:** Avoiding screens in the morning can help regulate your sleep patterns, leading to more restful nights.
4. **Stronger Relationships:** Spending less time on screens allows for more meaningful interactions with loved ones, strengthening your relationships.

5. **Increased Creativity:** With fewer digital distractions, your mind has more space for creative thinking and problem-solving.

Your Digital Detox Journey

Embarking on a morning digital detox is a journey that requires commitment and patience. Here are some steps to help you get started and stay on track:

1. **Set Clear Goals:** Define what you want to achieve with your digital detox. Whether it's reduced stress, improved focus, or better relationships, having clear goals keeps you motivated.
2. **Create a Routine:** Develop a morning routine that includes enjoyable, screen-free activities. Consistency is key to making the detox a habit.
3. **Monitor Your Progress:** Keep a journal or use an app to track your screen time and reflect on the benefits you're experiencing.
4. **Celebrate Successes:** Acknowledge and celebrate your progress, no matter how small. Each step forward is a victory.
5. **Stay Flexible:** Life can be unpredictable, so be flexible with your digital detox plans. If you slip up, don't get discouraged. Simply adjust and continue.

Unplug and Energize Your Morning with Digital Detox

Starting your day with a digital detox can transform your mornings and set you on the path to lifelong success. By reducing screen time, you can enjoy greater mental clarity, reduced stress, and improved relationships. Embrace the power of a screen-free morning and discover the benefits for yourself.

Your key to a focused start. Make every morning an opportunity to connect with yourself, your loved ones, and the world around you. Here's to a more mindful, focused, and fulfilling start to your day!

12 Mental Health: Building a Strong Foundation

Mental well-being, the gateway to a healthy life. In our fast-paced world, it's easy to overlook the importance of mental well-being. Yet, just as we prioritize physical health, nurturing our mental health is crucial for a balanced, fulfilling life. Today, we're diving into the topic of "Mental Health: Building a Strong Foundation," exploring practical steps to cultivate a resilient mind and create a solid foundation for lifelong success. So, grab a cup of your favorite calming tea, find a comfortable spot, and let's embark on this journey together!

Why Mental Health Matters

First, let's talk about why mental health is so important. Mental health influences how we think, feel, and act. It affects our ability to cope with stress, build relationships, and make decisions. A strong mental foundation is essential for:

1. **Emotional Resilience:** The ability to bounce back from setbacks and handle life's challenges with grace.
2. **Healthy Relationships:** Building and maintaining positive relationships with others.
3. **Productivity:** Staying focused and motivated in personal and professional endeavors.
4. **Overall Well-being:** Enhancing the quality of life and achieving a sense of fulfillment.

The Building Blocks of Mental Health

Just like building a house, creating a strong mental foundation requires certain building blocks. Here are the key components to focus on:

1. **Self-Awareness:** Understanding your emotions, thoughts, and behaviors is the first step toward improving mental health. Regular self-reflection helps you identify areas for growth and change.
2. **Healthy Habits:** Establishing routines that support mental well-being, such as regular exercise, a balanced diet, and sufficient sleep.
3. **Stress Management:** Learning techniques to manage stress effectively, such as mindfulness, deep breathing, and time management.
4. **Positive Relationships:** Surrounding yourself with supportive and uplifting people who encourage your growth and well-being.
5. **Professional Support:** Seeking help from mental health professionals when needed,

including therapists, counselors, and support groups.

Morning Rituals for Mental Health

Starting your day with practices that boost mental health can set a positive tone for the entire day. Here are some morning rituals to incorporate into your routine:

1. **Mindful Meditation:** Spend a few minutes each morning practicing mindfulness meditation. Focus on your breath and let go of any thoughts that arise. This practice can help reduce stress and increase self-awareness.
2. **Gratitude Journaling:** Write down three things you're grateful for each morning. This simple practice can shift your focus from what's wrong to what's right in your life, boosting your mood and promoting a positive outlook.
3. **Physical Activity:** Engage in some form of exercise, whether it's a brisk walk, yoga, or a workout. Physical activity releases endorphins, the body's natural mood lifters.
4. **Positive Affirmations:** Start your day with positive affirmations that reinforce your self-worth and capabilities. For example, "I am strong and capable," or "Today is a day full of opportunities."
5. **Healthy Breakfast:** Fuel your body with a nutritious breakfast that includes a balance of protein, healthy fats, and whole grains. A healthy diet is linked to better mental health.

Techniques for Building Emotional Resilience

Emotional resilience is the ability to adapt to stressful situations and bounce back from adversity. Here are some techniques to build and strengthen emotional resilience:

1. **Develop a Growth Mindset:** Embrace challenges as opportunities for growth rather than threats. A growth mindset fosters resilience by encouraging learning and perseverance.
2. **Practice Self-Compassion:** Be kind to yourself, especially during difficult times. Treat yourself with the same compassion you would offer a friend.
3. **Set Realistic Goals:** Break down your goals into manageable steps. Achieving small milestones can boost your confidence and motivation.
4. **Stay Connected:** Maintain strong connections with friends and family. Social support is crucial for resilience, providing comfort and perspective during tough times.
5. **Learn from Experience:** Reflect on past challenges and how you overcame them. Understanding your strengths and coping strategies can help you handle future difficulties.

Managing Stress Effectively

Stress is a natural part of life, but chronic stress can take a toll on mental health. Here are some strategies to manage stress effectively:

1. **Mindfulness Practices:** Engage in mindfulness activities like meditation, deep breathing, or yoga. These practices help calm the mind and reduce stress.

2. **Time Management:** Prioritize your tasks and break them into manageable chunks. Effective time management can prevent feelings of overwhelm.
3. **Relaxation Techniques:** Incorporate relaxation techniques such as progressive muscle relaxation, visualization, or aromatherapy into your routine.
4. **Stay Active:** Regular physical activity helps reduce stress hormones and promotes relaxation.
5. **Seek Support:** Talk to someone you trust about your stressors. Sometimes, sharing your feelings can provide relief and perspective.

Building Positive Relationships

Healthy relationships are a cornerstone of mental well-being. Here's how to build and maintain positive relationships:

1. **Communicate Openly:** Practice open and honest communication with others. Express your feelings and listen actively to others.
2. **Show Empathy:** Try to understand things from the other person's perspective. Empathy strengthens connections and fosters mutual respect.
3. **Set Boundaries:** Establish healthy boundaries to protect your well-being. It's okay to say no and prioritize your needs.
4. **Spend Quality Time:** Make time for the people who matter to you. Quality time strengthens bonds and creates lasting memories.
5. **Offer Support:** Be there for others when they need you. Providing support can strengthen

relationships and enhance your own sense of purpose.

Seeking Professional Help

Sometimes, despite our best efforts, we may need additional support. Seeking help from a mental health professional is a sign of strength, not weakness. Here are some options:

1. **Therapists and Counselors:** These professionals can help you navigate personal challenges, develop coping strategies, and improve mental health.
2. **Support Groups:** Joining a support group can provide a sense of community and shared experience, offering comfort and understanding.
3. **Helplines:** If you need immediate support, helplines can offer guidance and assistance in times of crisis.
4. **Online Resources:** Many online platforms offer mental health resources, including articles, videos, and virtual therapy sessions.

Real-Life Success Stories

Hearing from others who have prioritized their mental health can be incredibly inspiring. Here are a few real-life success stories:

1. **Richard, Entrepreneur:** "Building a strong mental foundation has been crucial for my business success. I start each day with meditation and gratitude journaling, which helps me stay focused and positive despite the challenges."
2. **Mike, Teacher:** "I used to feel overwhelmed by stress. Incorporating regular exercise and

mindfulness practices into my routine has made a significant difference. I'm more resilient and better equipped to handle my responsibilities."

3. **Pia, College Student:** "Seeking help from a counselor was the best decision I made. It gave me the tools to manage my anxiety and build healthier relationships. Now, I prioritize my mental health and feel more confident in my abilities."

Long-Term Benefits of Prioritizing Mental Health

Investing in your mental health offers long-term benefits that enhance your overall quality of life:

1. **Greater Emotional Stability:** Building a strong mental foundation helps you navigate life's ups and downs with greater ease and stability.
2. **Improved Physical Health:** Good mental health is linked to better physical health, including a stronger immune system and lower risk of chronic illnesses.
3. **Enhanced Relationships:** Healthy relationships are built on a foundation of strong mental health. Prioritizing your well-being improves your interactions with others.
4. **Increased Productivity:** Mental clarity and emotional resilience boost productivity and help you achieve your goals.
5. **Overall Happiness:** Prioritizing mental health leads to a greater sense of happiness and fulfillment in life.

Your Journey to Mental Wellness

Building a strong mental foundation is a journey that requires commitment and self-compassion. Here are some steps to help you get started and stay on track:

1. **Set Clear Intentions:** Define what mental wellness means to you and set clear intentions for your mental health journey.
2. **Create a Supportive Environment:** Surround yourself with positive influences and create an environment that supports your well-being.
3. **Practice Consistently:** Incorporate mental health practices into your daily routine. Consistency is key to building lasting habits.
4. **Reflect and Adjust:** Regularly reflect on your progress and make adjustments as needed. Be flexible and open to change.
5. **Celebrate Milestones:** Acknowledge and celebrate your achievements, no matter how small. Each step forward is a victory on your journey to mental wellness.

Kickstark Your Morning with Mental Wellness

Prioritizing your mental health is essential for a balanced and fulfilling life. By building a strong mental foundation, you can navigate life's challenges with resilience, maintain healthy relationships, and achieve your goals.

Nurture your mind and soul, and watch as you transform your mornings—and your life—into a journey of growth and success. Here's to a brighter, more balanced you!

13 Scribing—Reflecting the Planning

There is magic in writing - each stroke of the pen can help craft a day filled with purpose, goals with clarity, and a life of fulfillment. Scribing, or the act of writing things down, is a transformative practice that can help you reflect, plan, and set the stage for lifelong success. Today, we're diving into the topic of "Scribing—Reflecting the Planning," exploring how this simple yet powerful tool can enhance your mornings and overall well-being. So grab your favorite journal and a cup of coffee, and let's embark on this enlightening journey together!

The Power of Scribing

Scribing is more than just jotting down notes or making lists. It's a deliberate and reflective practice that allows you to capture your thoughts, ideas, and plans on paper. Here's why scribing is so powerful:

1. **Clarity and Focus:** Writing things down helps clarify your thoughts and focus on what's important. It transforms abstract ideas into concrete plans.
2. **Memory Enhancement:** Studies show that writing by hand improves memory and helps retain information better than typing.
3. **Emotional Release:** Journaling provides a safe space to express your feelings and emotions, which can be therapeutic and stress-relieving.
4. **Goal Setting and Tracking:** Scribing allows you to set clear goals and track your progress over time, keeping you accountable and motivated.
5. **Creative Expression:** Writing stimulates creativity and can lead to new insights and ideas.

Incorporating Scribing into Your Morning Routine

Integrating scribing into your morning routine can set a positive and productive tone for the rest of your day. Here's how to make scribing a part of your mornings:

1. **Set Aside Time:** Dedicate a specific time each morning for scribing. Even just 10-15 minutes can make a significant difference.
2. **Create a Comfortable Space:** Find a quiet, comfortable spot where you can write without

distractions. This could be at your kitchen table, a cozy chair, or even outside in your garden.

3. **Use the Right Tools:** Choose a journal or notebook that you enjoy using, and invest in a good pen. The right tools can make the experience more enjoyable and encourage consistency.
4. **Start with a Prompt:** If you're not sure where to begin, use prompts to guide your writing. Prompts like "What am I grateful for today?" or "What are my top three goals for the day?" can get your creative juices flowing.
5. **Be Consistent:** Make scribing a non-negotiable part of your morning routine. Consistency helps establish the habit and maximizes the benefits.

Scribing Techniques to Try

There are various scribing techniques you can explore to find what works best for you. Here are some popular methods:

1. **Morning Pages:** This technique, popularized by Julia Cameron's book "The Artist's Way," involves writing three pages of stream-of-consciousness thoughts first thing in the morning. It's a great way to clear your mind and spark creativity.
2. **Gratitude Journaling:** Start your day by writing down three things you're grateful for. This practice shifts your focus to the positive aspects of your life and boosts your mood.
3. **Goal Setting:** Write down your short-term and long-term goals. Break them into actionable steps and review your progress regularly.

4. **Reflection:** Reflect on your experiences, challenges, and successes. This can help you gain insights and learn from your past.
5. **Visualization:** Describe your ideal day, week, or year. Visualization helps manifest your goals and keeps you motivated.
6. **Affirmations:** Write down positive affirmations to reinforce self-belief and confidence. For example, "I am capable of achieving my goals," or "I am worthy of success."

Real-Life Success Stories

Hearing from others who have benefited from scribing can be incredibly motivating. Here are a few inspiring stories:

1. **Alice, Business Owner:** "I started journaling every morning to help manage the stress of running my own business. Writing down my goals and reflecting on my progress has kept me focused and motivated. It's amazing how much clarity and direction scribing has brought to my life."
2. **David, College Student:** "Balancing school, work, and personal life was overwhelming. I began using a journal to plan my day and set priorities. This simple habit has transformed my productivity and reduced my anxiety. I feel more in control and organized."
3. **Laura, Stay-at-Home Mom:** "As a mom, it's easy to lose sight of personal goals. I started a gratitude journal to remind myself of the positive aspects of each day. This practice has improved my mood and helped me find joy in the little things."

Overcoming Common Challenges

Starting a scribing practice can be challenging, especially if you're not used to writing regularly. Here are some tips to overcome common obstacles:

1. **Writer's Block:** If you're struggling to write, don't worry about perfection. Just start writing whatever comes to mind. Over time, the process will become more natural.
2. **Time Constraints:** If mornings are hectic, wake up a few minutes earlier or find a brief moment during breakfast to write. Even short sessions can be beneficial.
3. **Lack of Motivation:** Keep your journal visible and accessible. Sometimes, seeing it can remind you to write. You can also set reminders or prompts to stay motivated.
4. **Fear of Judgment:** Remember, your journal is for your eyes only. Write freely without worrying about grammar, spelling, or judgment. It's your personal space for reflection and growth.

Long-Term Benefits of Scribing

Incorporating scribing into your morning routine offers long-term benefits that can enhance your overall well-being and success:

1. **Improved Mental Health:** Regular journaling can reduce stress, anxiety, and depression by providing an outlet for emotions and thoughts.
2. **Enhanced Self-Awareness:** Writing helps you understand yourself better, identify patterns, and make informed decisions.

3. **Increased Productivity:** Setting clear goals and tracking progress keeps you focused and motivated, leading to greater productivity.
4. **Better Problem-Solving:** Reflecting on challenges and brainstorming solutions in your journal can improve your problem-solving skills.
5. **Greater Life Satisfaction:** Gratitude journaling and reflection practices can increase overall life satisfaction and happiness.

Making Scribing a Family Activity

Encouraging your family to join in on the scribing practice can be a fun and bonding experience. Here's how to make scribing a family activity:

1. **Family Journals:** Create a family journal where everyone can contribute their thoughts, goals, and reflections. This fosters communication and understanding.
2. **Journaling Time:** Set aside a specific time each morning for family journaling. This could be during breakfast or right after waking up.
3. **Shared Prompts:** Use shared prompts to guide the journaling process. For example, "What was the best part of your day yesterday?" or "What are you looking forward to today?"
4. **Encourage Creativity:** Allow family members to express themselves creatively in their journals through drawings, poems, or stories.
5. **Celebrate Together:** Celebrate milestones and achievements recorded in the journal as a family. This reinforces the habit and creates lasting memories.

Awake Your Potential with Scribing

Scribing is a powerful tool that can transform your mornings and set the stage for lifelong success. By incorporating this reflective practice into your daily routine, you can gain clarity, reduce stress, and stay focused on your goals.

The the habit of putting pen to paper and watch as your thoughts, plans, and dreams come to life. Here's to a brighter, more organized, and fulfilling day—one written word at a time!

14 SMART Goals: Setting Yourself Up for Success

Have you ever set a goal, only to find yourself losing motivation or direction halfway through? It happens to the best of us. But what if I told you there's a foolproof way to set and achieve your goals? Enter SMART goals—a tried-and-true method for creating clear, actionable, and attainable objectives. Today, we're diving into the world of SMART goals and how they can transform your mornings and set you on the path to lifelong success. So grab your favorite morning beverage, and let's get SMART about goal setting!

What Are SMART Goals?

SMART is an acronym that stands for Specific, Measurable, Achievable,

Relevant, and Time-bound. This framework helps you create goals that are clear, realistic, and trackable. Let's break down each component:

1. **Specific:** A goal should be clear and specific, leaving no room for ambiguity. Ask yourself the who, what, where, when, and why of your goal.
2. **Measurable:** Your goal should have criteria that allow you to track your progress. This helps you stay motivated and know when you've achieved your goal.
3. **Achievable:** Set a goal that is realistic and attainable, considering your current resources and constraints. It should challenge you but still be possible.
4. **Relevant:** Your goal should matter to you and align with your broader life objectives. It should be worthwhile and reflect your values and priorities.
5. **Time-bound:** Every goal needs a target date to create a sense of urgency and help you prioritize your tasks.

The Importance of Setting SMART Goals

Setting SMART goals is essential because it transforms vague intentions into actionable plans. Here's why SMART goals are so powerful:

1. **Clarity:** They provide a clear direction and focus, eliminating confusion and uncertainty.
2. **Motivation:** Breaking goals into measurable steps keeps you motivated and shows progress.
3. **Feasibility:** SMART goals ensure that your objectives are realistic and within your reach.

4. **Relevance:** They align your daily actions with your long-term aspirations.
5. **Accountability:** Time-bound goals create a sense of urgency and accountability, helping you stay on track.

How to Set SMART Goals

Ready to set your own SMART goals? Here's a step-by-step guide to help you get started:

1. **Identify Your Goal:** Think about what you want to achieve. Be specific and detail exactly what you want to accomplish.
2. **Make It Measurable:** Determine how you will measure your progress. Define clear criteria or indicators of success.
3. **Ensure It's Achievable:** Assess your resources and constraints. Ensure your goal is realistic given your current situation.
4. **Check Its Relevance:** Reflect on why this goal matters to you. Ensure it aligns with your broader life goals and values.
5. **Set a Deadline:** Establish a timeline for achieving your goal. Specify a target date or timeframe to create a sense of urgency.

Examples of SMART Goals

Let's look at some examples of SMART goals to see how this framework works in practice:

1. **Fitness Goal:**
   - Specific: "I want to run a 5K race."
   - Measurable: "I will track my running distance and time using a fitness app."

- Achievable: "I will start with a beginner's running plan and gradually increase my distance."
- Relevant: "Running a 5K will improve my fitness and overall health."
- Time-bound: "I will run the 5K race within three months."

2. **Career Goal:**
    - Specific: "I want to get a promotion to a senior manager position."
    - Measurable: "I will complete three leadership training courses and take on two new projects."
    - Achievable: "I will discuss my career goals with my supervisor and seek mentorship."
    - Relevant: "This promotion will advance my career and align with my professional aspirations."
    - Time-bound: "I aim to achieve this promotion within one year."
3. **Personal Development Goal:**
    - Specific: "I want to read more books."
    - Measurable: "I will read at least one book per month."
    - Achievable: "I will set aside 30 minutes each day for reading."
    - Relevant: "Reading will expand my knowledge and improve my mental well-being."
    - Time-bound: "I will read 12 books by the end of the year."

Tips for Achieving SMART Goals

Setting SMART goals is just the beginning. Here are some tips to help you stay on track and achieve your objectives:

1. **Break It Down:** Divide your goal into smaller, manageable tasks. This makes it less overwhelming and more attainable.
2. **Stay Organized:** Use tools like calendars, planners, or apps to keep track of your progress and deadlines.
3. **Monitor Progress:** Regularly review your progress and adjust your plan as needed. Celebrate small milestones to stay motivated.
4. **Seek Support:** Share your goals with friends, family, or mentors. Having a support system can provide encouragement and accountability.
5. **Stay Flexible:** Be open to adjusting your goals if necessary. Life is unpredictable, and flexibility can help you navigate obstacles.

Real-Life Success Stories

Hearing from others who have successfully used SMART goals can be inspiring. Here are a few real-life stories:

1. **Emma, Marketing Specialist:** "I wanted to improve my public speaking skills to advance my career. I set a SMART goal to join a local Toastmasters club and give six speeches within six months. Tracking my progress and receiving feedback helped me gain confidence and achieve my goal."
2. **Liam, Fitness Enthusiast:** "I set a goal to lose 15 pounds in three months by following a

SMART plan. I tracked my calorie intake, exercised five times a week, and kept a food journal. Breaking the goal into smaller tasks made it manageable, and I successfully reached my target weight."

3. **Sophia, College Student:** "Balancing school and work was challenging, so I set a SMART goal to improve my time management. I created a weekly schedule, set specific study hours, and aimed to complete all assignments two days before the deadline. This strategy helped me improve my grades and reduce stress."

Overcoming Challenges

Achieving SMART goals isn't always smooth sailing. Here's how to overcome common challenges:

1. **Procrastination:** Break your goal into smaller tasks and set mini-deadlines. Use techniques like the Pomodoro method to stay focused and productive.
2. **Lack of Motivation:** Remind yourself why the goal is important to you. Visualize the benefits of achieving it and reward yourself for progress.
3. **Unexpected Obstacles:** Stay flexible and adapt your plan as needed. Seek support from others and maintain a positive attitude.
4. **Fear of Failure:** Embrace failure as a learning opportunity. Reflect on what went wrong, make adjustments, and keep moving forward.

The Long-Term Benefits of SMART Goals

Setting and achieving SMART goals offers long-term benefits that go beyond the immediate sense of accomplishment:

1. **Increased Confidence:** Achieving your goals boosts self-confidence and reinforces your belief in your abilities.
2. **Better Time Management:** SMART goals improve your ability to prioritize tasks and manage your time effectively.
3. **Enhanced Problem-Solving Skills:** The process of setting and pursuing SMART goals hones your problem-solving and critical thinking skills.
4. **Greater Life Satisfaction:** Accomplishing meaningful goals contributes to overall life satisfaction and well-being.
5. **Continued Growth:** Setting SMART goals fosters a growth mindset, encouraging continuous learning and self-improvement.

Making SMART Goals a Family Activity

Encouraging your family to set and achieve SMART goals can be a fun and bonding experience. Here's how to make it a family activity:

1. **Family Meetings:** Hold regular family meetings to discuss individual and collective goals. Share progress and support each other.
2. **Shared Goals:** Set shared goals that everyone can work toward, such as planning a family vacation or starting a new hobby together.
3. **Celebrate Achievements:** Celebrate each other's successes, no matter how small. Recognize and reward progress to keep everyone motivated.

4. **Goal Charts:** Create a visual goal chart for the family. Track progress and update it regularly to keep everyone engaged.
5. **Lead by Example:** Demonstrate the importance of setting and achieving goals by actively pursuing your own SMART goals.

Your Game Changer with SMART Goals

Setting SMART goals is a powerful way to transform your mornings and set yourself up for lifelong success. By creating clear, actionable, and attainable objectives, you can achieve your dreams and lead a more focused, motivated, and fulfilling life.

Step into your potential with this game changing goal-setting framework and watch yourself achieve your dreams. Here's to a future brimming with success-one SMART goal at a time!

15 Creating Your Custom Morning Routine

The way you kick off your day has the power to influence everything that come in your life. Crafting a personalized morning routine can be your secret weapon for success, happiness, and productivity. Today, we're diving into the art of creating a custom morning routine that fits your unique lifestyle and goals. So grab a cup of your favorite morning drink, get comfy, and let's design the perfect start to your day together!

Why Morning Routines Matter

Before we get into the nitty-gritty of crafting your routine, let's talk about why morning routines are so powerful:

1. **Consistency:** A morning routine helps create consistency in your life, which can lead to better habits and improved discipline.
2. **Productivity:** Starting your day with purpose and intention can boost your productivity and help you accomplish more.
3. **Mental Clarity:** A well-planned morning routine can clear your mind, reduce stress, and set a positive tone for the day.
4. **Self-Care:** Morning routines provide dedicated time for self-care, helping you prioritize your well-being.

Step-by-Step Guide to Creating Your Custom Morning Routine

Creating a morning routine that works for you involves some experimentation and personalization. Here's a step-by-step guide to help you get started:

1. **Assess Your Current Mornings:** Reflect on your current morning habits. What's working for you, and what's not? Identifying your pain points can help you design a more effective routine.
2. **Set Clear Intentions:** Define what you want to achieve with your morning routine. Whether it's increased productivity, better health, or more relaxation, having clear goals will guide your routine.
3. **Prioritize Key Activities:** Choose a few key activities that align with your intentions. These could include exercise, meditation, reading, journaling, or planning your day. Focus on activities that energize and inspire you.

4. **Determine the Right Timing:** Decide how much time you want to dedicate to your morning routine. It could be 30 minutes or two hours—choose what fits your schedule. Start with a realistic timeframe and adjust as needed.
5. **Create a Sequence:** Arrange your chosen activities in a logical sequence. For example, you might start with stretching, followed by meditation, then breakfast, and end with planning your day. A consistent order helps build a habit.
6. **Prepare the Night Before:** Set yourself up for success by preparing the night before. Lay out your workout clothes, prepare your breakfast ingredients, or set up your meditation space. This reduces decision-making in the morning.
7. **Experiment and Adjust:** Give your routine a try and observe how it feels. Don't be afraid to tweak and adjust based on what works best for you. Flexibility is key to finding the perfect routine.

Elements of a Great Morning Routine

Let's explore some activities you might include in your morning routine. Remember, the best routine is one that fits your lifestyle and goals.

1. **Wake Up Early:** Give yourself ample time in the morning by waking up early. This peaceful time can be incredibly productive and set a calm tone for the day.
2. **Hydrate:** Start your day with a glass of water to rehydrate your body and kickstart your metabolism. Add a slice of lemon for an extra boost.

3. **Exercise:** Incorporate some form of physical activity to get your blood flowing. This could be a brisk walk, yoga, stretching, or a full workout. Exercise boosts energy and improves mood.
4. **Mindfulness or Meditation:** Spend a few minutes in mindfulness or meditation to center yourself. Focus on your breath, set positive intentions, and embrace the present moment.
5. **Healthy Breakfast:** Fuel your body with a nutritious breakfast. Choose balanced options that include protein, healthy fats, and whole grains to keep you energized throughout the morning.
6. **Journaling:** Reflect on your thoughts, set goals, or practice gratitude through journaling. This can help clear your mind and focus on what's important.
7. **Planning:** Review your schedule and set priorities for the day. Use a planner or digital calendar to organize your tasks and ensure you're on track.
8. **Personal Development:** Dedicate time to personal growth activities like reading, learning a new skill, or listening to a podcast. This stimulates your mind and encourages continuous learning.

Real-Life Success Stories

Hearing from others who have successfully created their own morning routines can be incredibly inspiring. Here are a few real-life stories:

1. **Oliver, Software Developer:** "I used to start my day feeling rushed and stressed. I decided to wake up an hour earlier and dedicate time to exercise and journaling. This simple change has significantly improved my productivity and overall mood. I feel more in control of my day."
2. **Sophie, Nurse:** "Working night shifts made it challenging to find a consistent routine. I created a flexible morning routine that includes stretching, a healthy breakfast, and a brief meditation. Even on busy days, these activities help me stay grounded and energized."
3. **Carlos, Entrepreneur:** "Running a business is demanding, so I needed a morning routine to stay focused. I start my day with a 20-minute workout, followed by planning and goal-setting. This routine has been a game-changer for my productivity and stress management."

Overcoming Common Challenges

Creating a morning routine isn't always smooth sailing. Here are some tips to overcome common challenges:

1. **Difficulty Waking Up Early:** Gradually adjust your wake-up time by 10-15 minutes each day until you reach your desired time. Ensure you're getting enough sleep by establishing a consistent bedtime.
2. **Lack of Time:** If mornings are hectic, start with a shorter routine and gradually expand it. Focus on high-impact activities that provide the most benefit.

3. **Staying Consistent:** Keep your routine visible by using reminders or setting alarms. Track your progress in a journal or app to stay motivated.
4. **Adapting to Changes:** Life is unpredictable, so be flexible with your routine. If something isn't working, adjust it. The goal is to create a routine that supports your well-being, not to add stress.

Making Your Routine a Family Affair

Incorporating your family into your morning routine can be a fun and bonding experience. Here's how to make it a family affair:

1. **Family Exercise:** Plan morning workouts or outdoor activities that everyone can enjoy. This promotes physical health and family bonding.
2. **Shared Breakfast:** Prepare and enjoy a healthy breakfast together. This creates a positive start to the day and encourages healthy eating habits.
3. **Mindfulness Together:** Practice mindfulness or meditation as a family. This can be a calming way to start the day and teach children the importance of mental well-being.
4. **Goal Setting:** Discuss and set individual or family goals during breakfast. This fosters communication and supports each other's aspirations.
5. **Reading Time:** Spend a few minutes reading together. Choose a family-friendly book or let each person read their own. This promotes a love for reading and personal development.

The Long-Term Benefits of a Custom Morning Routine

Establishing a custom morning routine offers long-term benefits that can transform your life:

1. **Increased Productivity:** A well-structured morning sets a productive tone for the day, helping you accomplish more.
2. **Better Mental Health:** Activities like exercise, mindfulness, and journaling reduce stress and improve overall mental health.
3. **Enhanced Physical Health:** Regular physical activity and a healthy breakfast contribute to better physical health and energy levels.
4. **Stronger Relationships:** Shared morning activities can strengthen family bonds and improve communication.
5. **Personal Growth:** Dedicating time to personal development activities fosters continuous learning and self-improvement.

Your Journey to a Better Morning

Creating a custom morning routine is a journey of self-discovery and improvement. Here are some steps to help you get started and stay on track:

1. **Start Small:** Begin with a few key activities and gradually build your routine. Consistency is more important than complexity.
2. **Be Patient:** It takes time to establish a new habit. Be patient with yourself and stay committed to your routine.
3. **Reflect and Adjust:** Regularly reflect on how your routine is working for you. Make

adjustments as needed to ensure it continues to meet your needs and goals.

4. **Celebrate Progress:** Acknowledge and celebrate your successes, no matter how small. Each step forward is a victory.
5. **Stay Inspired:** Seek inspiration from others who have successfully created their own routines. Learn from their experiences and adapt their strategies to fit your lifestyle.

Unfuck your Morning with a Custom Morning Routine

Creating a custom morning routine is a powerful way to transform your mornings and set yourself up for lifelong success. By designing a routine that fits your unique lifestyle and goals, you can start each day with purpose, energy, and positivity.

The activities that energize and inspire you, and watch as your mornings—and your life—become more fulfilling and productive. Here's to a brighter, more successful future.

16

The 30 Day Challenge: Transform Your Mornings, Transform Your Life

Are you ready to transform your mornings and, ultimately, your life? Enter the 30-Day Challenge—a powerful tool to help you build new habits, break old ones, and discover what works best for you. Today, we're diving into the exciting world of 30-day challenges, exploring how committing to small changes for just a month can lead to lasting success. So, grab your favorite morning beverage, get comfortable, and let's embark on this transformative journey together!

What is a 30-Day Challenge?

A 30-day challenge is a short-term commitment to a specific goal or habit for one month. The idea is to focus on one change at a time, making it manageable and achievable. Whether you want to start a new habit, break an old one, or simply try something new, a 30-day challenge is the perfect way to kickstart your transformation.

Why 30 Days?

You might wonder why 30 days is the magic number. Here's why a month-long commitment is so effective:

1. **Manageable Timeframe:** One month is long enough to see results but short enough to feel achievable. It's a perfect balance.
2. **Habit Formation:** Research suggests it takes about 21 to 30 days to form a new habit, making a 30-day challenge ideal for creating lasting changes.
3. **Focus and Commitment:** A specific timeframe helps you stay focused and committed, providing a clear start and end point.
4. **Visible Progress:** Within 30 days, you can see tangible progress, which boosts motivation and encourages you to keep going.

How to Choose Your 30-Day Challenge

Choosing the right challenge is key to your success. Here's a step-by-step guide to help you select a goal that resonates with you:

1. **Reflect on Your Goals:** Think about what you want to achieve. It could be related to health, productivity, self-care, learning, or any other area of your life.

2. **Identify One Specific Goal:** Focus on one goal at a time to avoid feeling overwhelmed. Make sure it's specific and clear.
3. **Ensure It's Achievable:** Choose a goal that's realistic and attainable within 30 days. It should challenge you but still be possible.
4. **Align with Your Values:** Pick a goal that aligns with your values and long-term aspirations. It should be meaningful and motivating.
5. **Prepare and Plan:** Plan how you'll incorporate the challenge into your daily routine. Gather any resources or support you might need.

Examples of 30-Day Challenges

Not sure where to start? Here are some inspiring 30-day challenge ideas to consider:

1. **Health and Fitness:**

   Daily Exercise: Commit to 30 minutes of exercise each day. This could be anything from walking to yoga to strength training.

   Healthy Eating: Try eating a balanced, nutritious meal every day. Focus on whole foods and cut out processed items.

   Hydration: Drink at least eight glasses of water daily.

2. **Productivity:**

   Morning Routine: Establish a morning routine that includes activities like meditation, journaling, and planning your day.

   Declutter: Spend 15 minutes each day decluttering a specific area of your home.

Read: Read for 20 minutes every day. Choose books that inspire and educate you.

3. **Self-Care:**

   Gratitude Journaling: Write down three things you're grateful for each day.

   Mindfulness: Practice mindfulness or meditation for 10 minutes daily.

   Digital Detox: Reduce screen time by setting specific limits on social media and other digital activities.

4. **Learning and Growth:**

   Learn a New Skill: Dedicate time each day to learning a new skill or hobby, such as playing an instrument or speaking a new language.

   Creative Writing: Write a short story, poem, or journal entry every day.

   Listen to Podcasts: Listen to educational or motivational podcasts during your commute or while doing chores.

Real-Life Success Stories

Hearing from others who have completed 30-day challenges can be incredibly motivating. Here are a few inspiring stories:

1. **Jake, Fitness Enthusiast:** "I decided to commit to a 30-day running challenge. I started with short runs and gradually increased my distance. By the end of the month, I felt stronger and more energized. It was amazing to see how much progress I made in just 30 days."

2. **Emily, Writer:** "As a writer, I often struggled with consistency. I took on a 30-day writing challenge, committing to write at least 500 words each day. This practice not only improved my writing skills but also boosted my creativity and discipline."

3. **Carlos, Entrepreneur:** "I wanted to improve my productivity, so I created a 30-day morning routine challenge. Each morning, I spent time meditating, journaling, and planning my day. This routine transformed my mornings and significantly increased my productivity and focus."

Tips for Success

To make the most of your 30-day challenge, keep these tips in mind:

1. **Start Small:** Choose a manageable goal to avoid feeling overwhelmed. Small, consistent actions lead to big changes over time.
2. **Track Your Progress:** Keep a journal or use an app to track your daily progress. Seeing your achievements can boost motivation and help you stay accountable.
3. **Stay Flexible:** Life is unpredictable, so be prepared to adapt. If you miss a day, don't get discouraged. Simply pick up where you left off and keep going.
4. **Find Support:** Share your challenge with friends or family members. Having a support system can provide encouragement and accountability.
5. **Celebrate Milestones:** Celebrate your achievements along the way. Recognize and reward your progress to stay motivated.

Overcoming Challenges

Every challenge comes with its own set of obstacles. Here's how to overcome common hurdles:

1. **Lack of Motivation:** Remind yourself why you started the challenge. Visualize the benefits and how achieving your goal will make you feel.
2. **Time Constraints:** Find pockets of time in your day to work on your challenge. Even small efforts can add up over 30 days.
3. **Unexpected Setbacks:** Stay flexible and adaptable. If something unexpected happens, adjust your plan and keep moving forward.
4. **Self-Doubt:** Replace negative thoughts with positive affirmations. Believe in your ability to achieve your goal.

The Long-Term Benefits of 30-Day Challenges

Completing a 30-day challenge offers long-term benefits that go beyond the immediate sense of accomplishment:

1. **Improved Discipline:** Committing to a daily practice builds discipline and self-control, which can be applied to other areas of your life.
2. **Greater Confidence:** Achieving your goals boosts self-confidence and reinforces your belief in your abilities.
3. **New Habits:** A 30-day challenge can help you establish new, positive habits that stick long after the challenge is over.
4. **Personal Growth:** Trying new things and pushing yourself out of your comfort zone

promotes personal growth and development.

5. **Enhanced Well-Being:** Depending on the challenge, you may experience physical, mental, or emotional benefits that enhance your overall well-being.

Making 30-Day Challenges a Family Activity

Involving your family in 30-day challenges can be a fun and bonding experience. Here's how to make it a family affair:

1. **Choose a Group Challenge:** Pick a challenge that everyone can participate in, such as a daily walk, healthy eating, or a gratitude practice.
2. **Set Common Goals:** Establish shared goals and work together to achieve them. This fosters teamwork and support.
3. **Create a Challenge Chart:** Use a visual chart to track everyone's progress. Update it daily to keep everyone engaged and motivated.
4. **Celebrate Together:** Celebrate milestones and successes as a family. Plan a special reward or activity to mark the end of the challenge.
5. **Share Experiences:** Hold regular family meetings to discuss the challenge. Share experiences, challenges, and successes to stay connected and inspired.

Revamp Your Routine with the 30-Day Challenge

A 30-day challenge is a powerful way to transform your mornings and set yourself up for lifelong success. By committing to small, consistent actions for one month, you can build new habits, achieve your goals, and experience lasting change.

Choose a goal that excites and motivates you, and watch as your mornings—and your life—transform in just 30 days. Here's to a brighter, more successful future, one day at a time!

17 The Lifelong Journey

Every morning is a blank slate have you ever paused to realize the power it holds to redefine your destiny? Let us dive into "The Life Long Journey," exploring how to embrace every day with purpose, passion, and a sense of adventure. Yourself Settle, and let's embark on this journey together!

Embracing the Journey

Life is not a destination; it's a journey filled with ups and downs, twists and turns. Every morning offers a chance to set the tone for your day and, ultimately, your life. Here's why it's important to embrace the journey:

1. **Personal Growth:** Every experience, whether good or

bad, contributes to your personal growth. Embracing the journey helps you learn and evolve continuously.

2. **Mindfulness:** Living in the moment allows you to appreciate the beauty and richness of life. Mindfulness helps reduce stress and increases happiness.
3. **Resilience:** Viewing life as a journey helps you navigate challenges with resilience and grace. It's about the process, not just the outcome.
4. **Fulfillment:** Embracing the journey leads to a more fulfilling life. It's about finding joy in the journey itself, not just in reaching the destination.

Setting Intentions

Each day is an opportunity to set intentions that guide your actions and decisions. Intentions are different from goals; they are about your attitude and approach to life. Here's how to set powerful intentions:

1. **Reflect:** Take a few moments each morning to reflect on what you want to bring into your day. Think about how you want to feel and what you want to focus on.
2. **Be Specific:** Make your intentions clear and specific. For example, "I intend to approach my work with creativity and enthusiasm" or "I intend to practice patience and kindness."
3. **Write Them Down:** Writing down your intentions helps solidify them in your mind. Keep them visible throughout the day as a reminder.

4. **Stay Flexible:** Life is unpredictable, and it's important to stay flexible. If things don't go as planned, adapt your intentions and keep moving forward.

Celebrating Small Wins

On this lifelong journey, it's important to celebrate the small wins along the way. Acknowledging your progress boosts motivation and confidence. Here's how to make celebrating small wins a part of your routine:

1. **Set Milestones:** Break down your goals into smaller milestones. Each milestone is a step towards your larger goal and deserves to be celebrated.
2. **Acknowledge Effort:** Celebrate the effort you put in, not just the outcome. Recognize your hard work and dedication.
3. **Reward Yourself:** Treat yourself to something enjoyable when you reach a milestone. It could be something simple like a relaxing bath, a favorite snack, or a fun outing.
4. **Share Your Success:** Share your achievements with friends or family. Celebrating together makes the journey more enjoyable and meaningful.

Learning from Challenges

Challenges and setbacks are inevitable on the lifelong journey. They are opportunities for growth and learning. Here's how to turn challenges into valuable lessons:

1. **Shift Your Perspective:** View challenges as opportunities rather than obstacles. Ask

yourself, "What can I learn from this experience?"

2. **Stay Positive:** Maintain a positive attitude, even in difficult times. Positivity helps you stay resilient and focused on finding solutions.
3. **Seek Support:** Don't be afraid to ask for help. Friends, family, or mentors can provide valuable support and perspective.
4. **Reflect and Adapt:** Reflect on what worked and what didn't. Adapt your approach and use the lessons learned to move forward stronger and wiser.

Cultivating Gratitude

Gratitude is a powerful practice that enhances your journey. It shifts your focus from what's lacking to what's abundant in your life. Here's how to cultivate gratitude:

1. **Gratitude Journaling:** Write down three things you're grateful for each day. This simple practice can transform your mindset and increase happiness.
2. **Express Thanks:** Take time to express gratitude to others. A heartfelt thank you can strengthen relationships and spread positivity.
3. **Mindful Appreciation:** Practice mindfulness by appreciating the small moments in your day. Whether it's a beautiful sunrise or a kind gesture, take time to savor it.
4. **Focus on Positives:** In challenging times, focus on what's going right. Gratitude helps you find silver linings and maintain a positive outlook.

Finding Your Passion

Passion fuels your journey and gives it meaning. Finding and pursuing your passions brings joy and fulfillment. Here's how to discover and nurture your passions:

1. **Explore Interests:** Try new activities and explore different interests. Pay attention to what excites and energizes you.
2. **Follow Curiosity:** Let your curiosity guide you. Ask questions, seek knowledge, and be open to new experiences.
3. **Reflect on Joy:** Think about times when you felt truly happy and engaged. What were you doing? These moments can provide clues to your passions
4. **Make Time:** Prioritize your passions and make time for them in your daily life. Pursuing what you love brings balance and satisfaction.

The Power of Reflection

Reflection is a crucial part of the lifelong journey. It helps you learn from the past, appreciate the present, and plan for the future. Here's how to incorporate reflection into your routine:

1. **Daily Reflection:** Spend a few minutes each evening reflecting on your day. What went well? What could be improved? What did you learn?
2. **Weekly Review:** At the end of each week, review your progress towards your goals. Celebrate achievements and adjust your plans as needed.

3. **Monthly Check-In:** Take a deeper dive into your progress and intentions each month. Reflect on your growth and set new intentions for the month ahead.
4. **Yearly Reflection:** At the end of the year, review your journey. Celebrate your achievements, reflect on lessons learned, and set goals for the new year.

Embracing Change

Change is a constant on the lifelong journey. Embracing change with an open mind and heart can lead to new opportunities and growth. Here's how to navigate change:

1. **Stay Open-Minded:** Be open to new experiences and perspectives. Embrace change as a chance to learn and grow.
2. **Adapt and Evolve:** Life is dynamic, and so are you. Adapt your plans and goals as needed to align with changing circumstances.
3. **Focus on Growth:** View change as a catalyst for personal growth. Each change brings new lessons and opportunities.
4. **Maintain Flexibility:** Stay flexible in your approach. Flexibility allows you to navigate change with resilience and ease.

Rise and Shine on Your Lifelong Journey

The lifelong journey is filled with opportunities for growth, joy, and fulfillment. By embracing each day with purpose, setting clear intentions, celebrating small wins, and learning from challenges, you can transform your mornings and your life.

Immerse yourself in the journey, uncover happiness in every step, and design a life rich accomplishment and joy. Here's to a brighter, more fulfilling future—one day at a time!

18 Real-Life Stories of Famous Personalities Who Transformed Their Lives by Starting Their Day Early

Tim Cook – CEO of Apple: The Power of Early Mornings

Tim Cook, the CEO of Apple, is renowned for his disciplined and early morning routine, which has played a significant role in his professional success and personal well-being. Cook's commitment to starting his day before dawn exemplifies how early mornings can transform one's life.

The Start of the Day: 3:45 a.m.

Tim Cook's alarm goes off at 3:45 a.m., a time when most of the world is still asleep. This early start gives him a significant head start on the day, allowing him to accomplish critical tasks without the distractions that typically come later.

1. **Emails and Communication:**

   By 4:00 a.m., Cook is already tackling his inbox. He begins his day by reading and responding to emails from colleagues and customers. This practice ensures that he is always in touch with the latest developments and feedback, allowing him to address issues promptly. Cook's dedication to staying connected helps maintain Apple's high standards of customer service and internal communication.

2. **Physical Fitness:**

   After handling his emails, Cook prioritizes his physical health with a workout. He is known to frequent a private gym where he engages in rigorous exercise routines. Physical fitness is a crucial part of Cook's daily regimen, providing him with the energy and mental clarity needed to lead one of the world's most influential tech companies. Exercise also helps him manage the stress that comes with his high-pressure role.

3. **Preparation and Planning:**

   By the time most people are waking up, Cook has already completed a significant portion of his day. He uses the early hours for deep thinking and strategic planning. This uninterrupted time allows him to focus on long-term goals and complex problems without the constant interruptions that occur during regular business hours.

The Impact of an Early Start

Tim Cook's early morning routine has several profound impacts on his professional life and the operations of Apple:

1. **Enhanced Productivity:**

   By starting his day early, Cook can handle critical tasks before the regular workday begins. This head start increases his overall productivity and allows him to be more proactive rather than reactive. His early start ensures that by the time the rest of the world is catching up, he has already made significant progress on his tasks.

2. **Strategic Focus:**

   The quiet morning hours provide Cook with the perfect environment for strategic thinking. Without the usual distractions, he can focus on big-picture ideas and innovations that drive Apple's success. This focus is essential for maintaining Apple's position at the forefront of technology and design.

3. **Work-Life Balance:**

   Despite his demanding schedule, Cook's early routine helps him maintain a better work-life balance. By completing key tasks early, he can allocate time later in the day for other important activities and personal interests. This balance is vital for long-term sustainability in a high-stress role.

Lessons from Tim Cook's Routine

Tim Cook's early morning habits offer valuable lessons for anyone looking to enhance their productivity and well-being:

1. **Discipline and Consistency:**

   Cook's routine underscores the importance of discipline and consistency. By waking up at the same time every day, he creates a stable and predictable schedule that maximizes productivity.

2. **Prioritizing Health:**

   Incorporating exercise into his morning routine shows the importance of prioritizing physical health. Regular exercise not only boosts energy levels but also improves mental clarity and resilience.

3. **Strategic Planning:**

   Using the early hours for strategic planning can help anyone, regardless of their profession, to focus on long-term goals and critical thinking. This approach can lead to better decision-making and innovation.

4. **Adaptability:**

   While Cook's routine is highly structured, it also reflects a level of adaptability. By preparing for the day ahead during the early hours, he can respond more effectively to unexpected challenges.

Conclusion

Tim Cook's transformation through his early morning routine is a testament to the power of starting the day with purpose and discipline. His ability to manage one of the world's most successful companies while maintaining personal well-being offers inspiration for anyone looking to enhance their life through early rising. By adopting similar habits, you too can set yourself up for success, productivity, and a balanced life. So, rise and shine, and take a page from Tim Cook's book to transform your mornings and your life!

Elon Musk – CEO of Tesla and SpaceX: The Early Riser Who Transforms Industries

Elon Musk, the CEO of Tesla and SpaceX, is one of the most influential and innovative entrepreneurs of our time. His ambitious ventures in electric vehicles, space travel, and artificial intelligence have revolutionized multiple industries. Central to his success is his disciplined and highly structured morning routine. Musk's commitment to starting his day early has played a significant role in his ability to juggle multiple high-stakes projects and maintain his visionary focus.

The Start of the Day: 5:00 a.m.

Elon Musk's alarm clock rings at 5:00 a.m., marking the beginning of his carefully orchestrated day. Waking up early allows Musk to maximize his productivity and maintain a rigorous schedule. Here's a detailed look at how his morning routine sets the stage for his extraordinary achievements:

1. **Immediate Productivity:**

   Musk is known for his intense work ethic, and his day starts immediately upon waking. He spends the first 30 minutes of his day reading and responding to critical emails. This early communication ensures that he is always in the loop and can address any urgent matters promptly. By tackling important correspondence first thing in the morning, Musk sets a proactive tone for the rest of the day.

2. **Prioritizing Tasks:**

   After handling his emails, Musk dedicates time to planning his day. He is a strong advocate of time-blocking, a technique where he schedules his day in five-minute increments. This method allows him to prioritize tasks and allocate his time efficiently. By meticulously planning his schedule, Musk can ensure that he focuses on high-impact activities and avoids wasting time.

3. **Family Time:**

   Despite his demanding schedule, Musk makes it a point to spend time with his family in the morning. He has breakfast with his children, which not only provides a moment of bonding but also a grounding start to his day. Balancing family time with his professional responsibilities is a priority for Musk, reflecting his commitment to maintaining personal connections despite his busy life.

4. **Physical Fitness:**

   Musk understands the importance of physical health in sustaining his intense work pace. Although he often admits that finding time for exercise can be challenging, he incorporates it into his routine whenever possible. His preferred forms of exercise include weightlifting and running, which help him stay fit and boost his energy levels.

5. **Strategic Thinking:**

   The early hours are also a time for Musk to engage in deep, strategic thinking. Whether it's envisioning the future of electric vehicles or planning the next mission to Mars, this quiet time allows him to focus on long-term goals and innovative ideas. This uninterrupted period is crucial for a visionary leader like

Musk, enabling him to think creatively and strategically.

The Impact of an Early Start

Elon Musk's early morning routine has several profound impacts on his professional life and the operations of his companies:

1. **Enhanced Productivity:**

   By starting his day early and employing time-blocking, Musk significantly increases his productivity. This disciplined approach ensures that he maximizes his output and efficiently handles the numerous responsibilities that come with leading multiple high-profile companies.

2. **Proactive Problem Solving:**

   Addressing emails and planning his day first thing in the morning allows Musk to be proactive rather than reactive. This proactive stance is essential for managing complex projects and navigating the challenges that arise in dynamic industries like technology and aerospace.

3. **Work-Life Balance:**

   Despite his intense work schedule, Musk's routine reflects a commitment to maintaining a work-life balance. By allocating time for family and physical fitness, he ensures that his personal well-being and relationships are not neglected.

4. **Innovative Thinking:**

   The early morning hours provide Musk with a quiet and focused environment for strategic thinking. This time is vital for generating innovative ideas and planning long-term strategies that drive the success of Tesla, SpaceX, and his other ventures.

Lessons from Elon Musk's Routine

Elon Musk's early morning habits offer valuable lessons for anyone looking to enhance their productivity and achieve their goals:

1. **Discipline and Structure:**

   Musk's disciplined approach to his morning routine, particularly his use of time-blocking, highlights the importance of structure in achieving high productivity. Planning your day in detail can help you prioritize tasks and stay focused.

2. **Proactive Start:**

   Starting the day by addressing important tasks and planning sets a proactive tone. Tackling critical issues early ensures that you are in control and can handle unexpected challenges effectively.

3. **Balancing Priorities:**

   Musk's commitment to family time and physical fitness underscores the importance of balancing professional and personal priorities. Taking care of your well-being and maintaining relationships are crucial for long-term success.

4. **Strategic Thinking:**

   Allocating quiet time for strategic thinking can lead to innovative ideas and long-term success. This practice is particularly valuable for leaders and entrepreneurs who need to stay ahead in competitive industries.

Conclusion

Elon Musk's transformation through his early morning routine is a testament to the power of starting the day with discipline and purpose. His ability to manage multiple groundbreaking projects while maintaining personal well-being offers inspiration for anyone looking to achieve extraordinary success. By adopting similar habits, you too can set yourself up for a productive and fulfilling life. So, rise and shine, and take a page from Elon Musk's book to transform your mornings and your life!

Richard Branson – Founder of Virgin Group: The Power of Early Mornings

Richard Branson, the charismatic founder of the Virgin Group, is a prominent example of how an early morning routine can transform one's life. With over 400 companies under the Virgin umbrella, Branson's ability to juggle multiple ventures while maintaining his adventurous lifestyle is truly remarkable. A significant part of his success is attributed to his disciplined habit of starting his day early.

The Start of the Day: 5:00 a.m.

Richard Branson's day begins at 5:00 a.m., a practice he believes gives him a head start on the day. Rising early allows him to engage in activities that boost his energy and focus, setting a positive tone for the rest of the day. Here's a detailed look at Branson's early morning routine and how it contributes to his success:

1. **Physical Activity:**

   Branson is a strong advocate of physical

fitness, and his mornings often start with exercise. He enjoys a variety of activities, including playing tennis, kitesurfing, swimming, and cycling. These workouts not only keep him in excellent physical shape but also invigorate his mind. Exercise is a natural stress reliever and mood booster, which is crucial for maintaining the high energy levels needed to manage his diverse business interests.

2. **Quality Family Time:**

   Despite his busy schedule, Branson values family time and incorporates it into his morning routine. He often has breakfast with his family, which provides a grounding start to his day. This practice helps strengthen family bonds and ensures that he remains connected to his loved ones, no matter how hectic his professional life gets.

3. **Reflection and Planning:**

   After his workout and family breakfast, Branson spends time reflecting and planning his day. This quiet time is essential for strategic thinking and goal setting. He reviews his to-do list, prioritizes tasks, and sets clear objectives for the day. This practice ensures that he stays focused and productive, aligning his daily activities with his long-term goals.

4. **Early Morning Work:**

   Branson also uses the early hours to tackle important work tasks. By starting his workday early, he can address critical emails and make strategic decisions before the usual business hours begin. This proactive approach allows him to stay ahead of his schedule and reduces the stress of dealing with urgent matters later in the day.

The Impact of an Early Start

Richard Branson's early morning routine has several profound impacts on his professional life and the operations of his companies:

1. **Enhanced Productivity:**

   Waking up early and engaging in physical activity boosts Branson's productivity. The combination of exercise and strategic planning in the morning helps him maintain high energy levels and stay focused throughout the day. This routine allows him to accomplish more in less time, making efficient use of his day.

2. **Positive Mindset:**

   Starting the day with activities he enjoys, such as exercise and family time, puts Branson in a positive mindset. This optimistic outlook is crucial for tackling the challenges of running a global business empire. A positive attitude not only enhances his performance but also influences his interactions with others, fostering a collaborative and motivated work environment.

3. **Work-Life Balance:**

   Despite his demanding career, Branson's routine reflects a commitment to work-life balance. By prioritizing family time and personal well-being, he ensures that his professional responsibilities do not overshadow his personal life. This balance is vital for long-term sustainability and happiness.

4. **Strategic Focus:**

   The early morning hours provide Branson with uninterrupted time for strategic thinking. This quiet period allows him to focus on big-picture ideas and long-term goals, driving innovation and growth within the Virgin Group. His ability to think creatively and strategically is a key factor in his success as an entrepreneur.

Lessons from Richard Branson's Routine

Richard Branson's early morning habits offer valuable lessons for anyone looking to enhance their productivity and achieve their goals:

1. **Discipline and Consistency:**

   Branson's commitment to waking up early and maintaining a consistent routine highlights the importance of discipline. Establishing a structured morning routine can help you stay focused and achieve your objectives more efficiently.

2. **Prioritizing Health:**

   Incorporating physical activity into your morning routine is essential for maintaining high energy levels and mental clarity. Exercise not only improves physical health but also enhances cognitive function and emotional well-being.

3. **Balancing Priorities:**

   Branson's routine demonstrates the importance of balancing professional and personal priorities. Making time for family and self-care is crucial for maintaining overall happiness and well-being.

4. **Strategic Planning:**

   Using the early hours for reflection and planning can help you stay organized and focused on your long-term goals. This practice ensures that your daily activities align with your broader vision and objectives.

Conclusion

Richard Branson's transformation through his early morning routine is a testament to the power of starting the day with discipline and purpose. His ability to manage a global business empire while maintaining personal well-being and a positive outlook offers inspiration for anyone looking to achieve extraordinary success. By adopting similar habits, you too can set yourself up for a productive and fulfilling life. So, rise and shine, and take a page from Richard Branson's book to transform your mornings and your life!

About the Author

Pranshu Anand is an Engineering Manager, writer, and a firm believer in the transformative power of mornings. An alumnus of the Indian Institute of Technology (IIT) Guwahati, he began his career as a Software Development Engineer at Amazon before taking a bold step—leaving his job to pursue the Civil Services Examination.

It was during this intense phase of preparation that Pranshu discovered the magic of mornings. Instead of burning the midnight oil, he adopted the habit of starting his day early, unlocking newfound focus, productivity, and clarity. Through this journey, he also rediscovered his love for writing, penning two works—one in Hindi and one in English—as he explored the connection between self-discipline and success.

Now working as an Engineering Manager at a multinational corporation, Pranshu continues to apply his passion for habit-building, discipline, and personal growth in both his professional and personal life. His book, Unfuck Morning Miracle Habits, is a testament to the life-changing power of a well-structured morning, inspiring readers to break free from chaotic routines and harness the limitless potential of the early hours.